East African Lessons on Economic Liberalization

This is the second title in the Thames Essay series, arising out of the Trade Policy Research Centre's programme on the Participation of Developing Countries in the International Trading System, supervised by Martin Wolf, the Centre's Director of Studies. The earlier title was

Myths and Reality of External Constraint on Development
by James Riedel

Other titles in the programme to be published as Thames Essays are provisionally entitled

Economic Impact of Generalized Tariff Preferences
by Rolf J. Langhammer and André Sapir

Impediments to Trade Liberalization in Sri Lanka
by Deepak Lal and Sarath Rajapatirana

Developing Countries in the GATT Legal System
by Robert Hudec

Impediments to Trade Liberalization in the Philippines
by Romeo Bautista

Thames Essay No. 48

East African Lessons on Economic Liberalization

BY

David Bevan

Arne Bigsten

Paul Collier

AND

Jan Willem Gunning

Gower

Aldershot · Brookfield USA · Hong Kong · Singapore · Sydney

for the

TRADE POLICY RESEARCH CENTRE

London

First published 1987 by

Gower Publishing Company Limited
Gower House, Croft Road, Aldershot, Hampshire GU11 3HR
United Kingdom

Gower Publishing Company
Old Post Road, Brookfield, Vermont 05036
United States of America

Gower Publishing Australia
85 Whiting Street, Artamon, New South Wales 2064,
Australia

ISSN 0306-6991
ISBN 0 566 05337 3

British Library Cataloguing-in-Publication Data
East African Lessons on Economic Liberalization
(Thames Essay No. 48)
1. Africa, East — Economic Conditions
I. Bevan, David II. Trade Policy Research Centre
III. Series
330.967'604 HC860

Library of Congress Cataloging-in-Publication Data
East African Lessons on Economic Liberalization
(Thames Essay No. 48)
Bibliography: p.67
1. Kenya — Commercial policy. 2. Tanzania — Commercial policy. 3. Economic Stabilization — Kenya. 4. Economic stabilization — Tanzania. 5. Industry and state — Kenya. 6. Industry and state — Tanzania. I. Bevan, David. II. Trade Policy Research Centre. III. Series.
HF1612.5.E37 1987 338.967 86-29602

Printed in the United Kingdom by
Biddles Ltd, Guildford, Surrey

Contents

List of Tables

The Authors

THE AUTHORS of this Thames Essay are members of the Unit for the Study of African Economies in the Institute of Economics and Statistics, University of Oxford, and have extensive research experience on East Africa.

DAVID BEVAN is a Fellow of St. John's College and a Research Associate at the Institute of Economics and Statistics, University of Oxford. ARNE BIGSTEN, a Visiting Associate of the Institute, is a Research Fellow in the Department of Economics at the University of Gothenburg in Sweden. PAUL COLLIER is a Fellow at St Antony's College and a University Lecturer in Economics at the University of Oxford. JAN WILLEM GUNNING is Director of the Economisch en Sociaal Instituut at the Free University of Amsterdam in the Netherlands.

Preface

RELATIONS between developed and developing countries in the international trading system, whose norms, rules and procedures are set out in the General Agreement on Tariffs and Trade (GATT), have been reaching an *impasse*. For quarter of a century, the developed countries have been allowing, or encouraging, the developing countries to become contracting parties to the GATT without requiring them to abide by the more important obligations of membership. What is more, they have acquiesced in the formal derogation from the principle of non-discrimination, which is the keystone of the GATT, to permit the Generalized System of Preferences (GSP) in favour of developing countries to be established and maintained.

At the same time, developing countries — especially the more advanced ones — have been faced with discriminatory protection against them whenever their exports have been uncomfortably successful in the markets of developed countries, such protection often taking the form of export-restraint arrangements negotiated 'outside' the framework of GATT norms, rules and procedures.

The costs to developing countries of limitations on their access to the markets of developed countries are not so much offset as multiplied by their more or less complete freedom to establish and maintain trade regimes which are highly protectionist and Byzantine in their complexity.

By the early 1980s, it was clear that the role of developing countries in the international trading system was bound to attract increasing attention, especially if a new 'round' of multilateral trade negotiations under GATT auspices was to be undertaken. Accordingly, the Trade Policy Research Centre, with the help of a grant from the Leverhulme Trust in London, embarked in 1983 on a major programme of studies on the Participation of Developing Countries in the International Trading System, supervised by Martin Wolf, the Centre's Director of Studies.

The purpose of the programme has been to clarify, for public discussion and policy formation, the underlying reasons for the current difficulties in relations between developed and developing countries in the GATT system. The programme focusses both on economic and legal issues in the GATT system *per se* and on impediments to trade liberalization in individual developing countries. The emphasis on the latter derived from the perception that the GATT framework of norms, rules and procedures can be no more than the 'handmaiden' of trade liberalization. Liberalization will not be brought about, however, unless there is a consensus in the countries concerned on both its feasibility and its value in promoting their economic growth and development. The domestic impediments to trade liberalization have to be understood if they are to be overcome.

It is true for all countries that multilateral negotiations are a means more of achieving the trade liberalization that is already widely understood to be in each country's own interests than of liberalizing when no such benefit is seen. In other words, reciprocal bargaining is a way of overcoming domestic resistance to the trade liberalization that is strongly desired by prevailing forces in each country, both in government and in society at large. A desire to liberalize, almost irrespective of what happens elsewhere, is particularly significant in small countries. The smaller the country, the less effective is its international bargaining power and, therefore, the less persuasive is the argument that improved access to markets abroad depends on the liberalization of access to its own market. For this reason, smaller countries usually liberalize only if there is a strong domestic consensus that such liberalization is in their own interests, such a consensus having been long established in countries like Sweden, Switzerland and Singapore.

From a trade policy point of view, almost all developing countries are small. Thus the use they can or will make of the international trading system depends, in the first place, on the strength of the domestic desire to liberalize and, in the second place, on the role that international bargaining can play in the process. It is with these questions in mind that a number of country studies have been undertaken as part of the Centre's programme. Apart from the study of Kenya and Tanzania reported in these pages, there are studies of the Republic of Korea, the Philippines and Sri Lanka in East Asia and of Argentina, Brazil and Colombia in Latin America.

Paul Collier and David Bevan, of the Institute of Economics and Statistics at the University of Oxford, Jan Gunning, of the Free University of Amsterdam, and Arne Bigsten, of the University of Gothenburg, have taken a special interest in the economies of East Africa. As they show in this Thames Essay, the case of Tanzania raises very special issues, but issues that are relevant to other highly controlled economies that are also dependent on peasant production of food and other crops for export, such economies as Burma, Ethiopia, Ghana, Madegascar and Mozambique. The problems of such countries are not so important to the GATT system, to which they are hardly relevant and which is, for the most part, of little relevance to them. They are more important to the international institutions directly concerned with them, mostly the World Bank and the International Monetary Fund, and to the promotion of economic development in general. Some of the world's poorest people live in these countries. Policies that improve their prospects therefore have great significance for global economic welfare.

It is widely agreed among economists who take a special interest in developing countries that one element of policy reform is the need to liberalize the economy. There is even a stirring of opinion in some of these countries that liberalization, if not desirable, is to some extent inescapable. Yet the distortions in their economies have become so pervasive and binding that the task of finding a liberalization path, one that is both politically and economically feasible, is very baffling. It is the chief merit of this study that it indicates why liberalization is both important and difficult in such cases. The study may be seen, then, as presenting an extreme case of the difficulties which have to be tackled when those countries try to end economic controls and thereby benefit from taking part more fully in the world economy.

Drafts of the papers arising from the Centre's programme of studies were presented at a three-day research meeting at Wiston House, near Steyning, in the United Kingdom, attended by those engaged on the programme and a number of other scholars and officials. The meeting was immediately preceded by a two-day meeting, also at Wiston House, of a study group which is drawing together the conclusions of the programme of studies. This meeting, too, was attended by a number of officials. The two international meetings were funded by a grant from the Ford Foundation in New York, while the programme of studies as a whole has been funded by the Leverhulme Trust in London.

The authors have been grateful for the extensive comments of Mr Wolf and for those, too, of Vincent Cable and I.M.D. Little, who were the discussants on their first draft at the Wiston House research meeting. They also acknowledge the help of Patrick Alila, H.K.R. Amani, Enos Bukuku, Benno Ndula and George Ruigu.

As usual, it has to be stressed that the views expressed in this Thames Essay do not necessarily represent those of members of the Council or those of the staff and associates of the Trade Policy Research Centre which, having general terms of reference, does not represent a consensus of opinion on any particular issue. The purpose of the Centre is to promote independent analysis and public discussion of international economic policy issues.

HUGH CORBET
Director
Trade Policy Research Centre

London
August 1986

Introduction

Martin Wolf

THE purpose of the programme of studies of which this study is a part has been to examine the obstacles to the increased participation of developing countries in the international trading system, as governed by the General Agreement on Tariffs and Trade (GATT). From quite early on, however, it was obvious that the principal obstacle to such participation was the inability and, indeed, the unwillingness of the countries concerned to contemplate a significant reduction in trade barriers. For this reason, a major part of the programme has been an examination of obstacles to trade liberalization, both political and economic, in a selected group of developing countries.

In order to obtain a balanced view of the problems involved it was thought useful to look at the situation of small African countries, even though their direct significance for the GATT system is but modest, as is the relevance to them of the GATT. By its nature, the reciprocal bargaining that is at the heart of the process of trade liberalization in the GATT framework is a game to be played by countries that have something to bargain with. Small countries must, willy nilly, accept whatever crumbs fall from the negotiators' table. This does not mean, however, that the negotiations are of little importance for them. A world of stable, liberal and non-discriminatory trade policy is probably still more important to small, weak and trade-dependent economies than to the greater powers. It is just that they can do little to help to bring it about.

What they can do is position themselves to exploit such opportunities as do arise. Unfortunately, the development of policy in many African economies has been in the opposite direction. A report from the World Bank has remarked:

> 'Since African economies are typically small and dependent on world trade, and since agriculture accounts for a large share of GDP and exports, two strategic pricing policies are critical: exchange rates and agricultural prices, both for food and commodity exports. There has been a general overvaluation of exchange rates. Exports have stagnated and have been unable to keep pace with rising imports. The internal terms of trade have shifted against agriculture during the 1970s, especially in the case of export crops. The growing scarcity of foreign exchange has been met by increasing resort to import licensing and exchange controls. By the early 1980s, many sub-Saharan African countries had active illegal markets in foreign exchange and in bartered goods. Devaluation of domestic currencies had, therefore, become an increasingly pressing need.[1]

By the early 1980s, the economic difficulties in which many African countries found themselves had led to quite widespread agreement not only in the major international institutions involved, principally the International Monetary Fund (IMF) and the World Bank, but even on the part of many governments that the line of analysis in the above quotation was essentially correct. Liberalization and associated improvements in the incentive structure were at least a part of the needed programme of economic reform. Since the growth of GDP per capita had been 0.7 per cent for Sub-Saharan Africa in the 1970s and was negative in the 1980s, it is not surprising that policy reform was thought to be needed.[2] Still worse, low-income Sub-Saharan African countries had experienced negative growth of GDP per capita even in the 1970s.[3] The living standards of a large number of the poorest people in the world were steadily deteriorating despite the copious rhetoric about economic development, the priority to be accorded to basic needs and so forth.

The main international interlocutors have been the IMF and the World Bank. Both agree that there needs to be an emphasis on stabilization and economic liberalization. Largely for institutional reasons, however, the programmes of the two institutions differ somewhat in emphasis. The IMF focuses largely (but not exclusively) on the need for devaluation and control of domestic credit expansion, which in turn usually requires reductions in the public-sector deficit.[4] These elements reflect the situation with which the IMF is usually confronted, namely an unsustainable deficit in the current account of the balance of payments. Furthermore, it is a natural consequence of the short pay-back periods for resources available from the IMF, especially stand-by arrangements, that the time horizon for adjustment is itself short.

By contrast, the objective of structural adjustment lending from the World Bank 'is to support...measures specifically designed to strengthen countries' balances of payments over the medium term (i.e., within a five-year to seven-year time frame)'.[5] Like the IMF, the World Bank, too, is interested in macro-economic policy, but, in addition, it pays attention to measures that affect the efficiency of resource use, especially trade liberalization, incentives for exports, domestic pricing policy, the allocation of public investment and increased institutional efficiency, particularly in the public sector.[6]

At the risk of caricature, the IMF tends to focus on getting demand 'right' in the short term and the World Bank on getting prices 'right' in the medium term. While real, these are differences of institutional predilection and function rather than of fundamental analysis, since the intellectual framework within which both institutions operate is that of neo-classical orthodoxy. Not surprisingly, the policy recommendations of both these institutions are controversial. Some critics dislike the emphasis on markets and the orthodox perspective on fiscal, monetary and trade policies. Others criticize the IMF, in particular, for its alleged indifference to the implications of its recommendations for income distribution. Yet others assert that the IMF is insufficiently aware of the political context in which its recommendations are to work.

These are important issues, not least from the perspective of the research programme sponsored by the Trade Policy Research Centre. One of the starting points for the programme was the desirability of economic liberalization in developing countries and the role international arrangements, principally the GATT, can play in achieving such liberalization. In the case of Sub-Saharan Africa, however, the principal vehicles for advice on how to liberalize are recommendations from, and negotiations with, the IMF and the World Bank. It is important, therefore, to feel confident that that advice is appropriate to the conditions in which it is applied. It is at this vital, but relatively technical, level that the study by David Bevan, Arne Bigsten, Paul Collier and Jan Willem Gunning makes its contribution.

It so happens that the scholarly literature contains interesting discussions of the relations between the IMF, in particular, and the two countries under consideration in the present study: Kenya and Tanzania. In his study of Kenya's experience between 1975 and 1981, Tony Killick, [7] of the Overseas Development Institute in London, points out that there were no fundamental conflicts of principle between Kenya and the IMF. He argues, therefore, that 'if successful stabilization and good working relationships are not feasible in Kenya, it is unclear where else in Africa they might be achieved'. In practice, however, conflicts did arise, but these tended to reflect differences over timing, with the Kenyans unhappy about the IMF's short-term outlook and, for that reason, relatively content with the approach taken by the World Bank.[8] The general presumption is that adjustment remedies based on orthodox economic analysis, if propertly and sensitively administered, would work in an economy like that of Kenya.

On this point the present study agrees. Despite failures in Kenyan policy, the authors conclude that 'piecemeal policy changes can succeed in liberalizing trade in the control regime found in Kenya, but they were liable to fail in the circumstances of the Tanzanian economy during the 1978-84 period'. The sharp distinction between the two cases and the nature of the lessons to be drawn from it is the central point of the essay.

It is interesting to note that another study of Tanzania had also concluded that the orthodox approach to the problems of Tanzania is fundamentally misconceived. Reginald Green, of the Institute of Development Studies at the University of Sussex, contrasts Tanzania's National Economic Survival Programme (NESP) of 1981 with the approach of the IMF as follows: 'The main NESP-IMF divergence is on the relative weights to be given to specific, contextual, micro measures (often physical and requiring allocation whether by nonmarket instruments or market intervention) and to macro, "free play of market forces" oriented measures.'[9] Dr Green strongly supports the approach of the NESP, which may be thought of as an attempt to use the traditional Tanzanian style of policy-making, but for the purposes of adjustment to enormous external imbalances.

From a very different analytical starting point, the present study suggests that orthodox remedies are, indeed, inappropriate in an economy like Tanzania. Just because the Tanzanians have proceeded so far with their peculiar approach to economic policy, the economy can no longer be expected to react normally. What for Dr Green is a recommendation becomes, from the perspective of the present study, a constraint.

The essential point of the analysis is that distortions created by pervasive rationing in an economy dependent on peasant agriculture are liable to provoke a perverse response to piecemeal improvements in incentives. As the authors note, 'by combining a decline in the terms of trade with a boom-inherited increase in government expenditure, a negative shock can create a switch of regime into rationing'. Once rationing is in effect some strange things can happen. In particular, peasants will be prepared to exchange cash crops for cash during a honeymoon period, because of the need to have means to purchase such consumer goods as may become available from time to time. After a while, however, peasants will cut back on their sales of cash crops since there is nothing of value for them to obtain in return. From the government's perspective the honeymoon period, when it was able to obtain something valuable (cash crops) for nothing (printed pieces of paper), turns into an unexpected and sudden divorce, when the peasants effectively cease to participate in the cash economy. Since the output of peasants is the main source of foreign exchange, the resulting foreign-exchange shortage tends to make the economy implode.

In such an economy, the authors argue, the response to orthodox policy changes like devaluation or a rise in the price of the cash crops may well be perverse. With abundant cash holdings and nothing to spend them on, rational peasants are quite likely to *reduce* sales of cash crops in response to improved prices. The authors argue that a satisfactory policy package would probably have to include both substantial aid-financed increases in the supply of consumer goods and a currency reconstruction, aimed at sterilizing a large part of the accumulated cash balances, in addition to such orthodox elements as devaluation. Without the improved availability of goods from abroad there would probably have to be a sharp squeeze on urban standards of living to release consumer goods to peasants; but such a squeeze may well be politically infeasible.

The problem is that when rationing begins to bite it is likely to create an initially favourable situation followed by a disaster. Furthermore, there is no simple way of avoiding that disaster. The design of a successful adjustment programme is a complex and politically difficult business. One is reminded of the story of the wayfarer who, upon asking the way to Dublin, receives the reply, 'If I were you, I wouldn't start from here'. The problem, the authors note, is that if a price-control apparatus is in place in a largely peasant economy that is also vulnerable to external shocks, one is all too likely to end up 'here' from time to time. The problems identified for Tanzania affect a number of economies now and are likely to affect still more in the future unless policies that may lead to rationing are eschewed.

Subsequent experience in Tanzania will indicate whether the authors are correct in their analysis of the situation of that country. In April 1986, President Mwinyi, who had taken over from President Nyerere in November 1985, authorized a devaluation from sixteen to 40 Tanzanian shillings to the American dollar, as well as large increases in producer prices. By this time the evidence for accelerating decline had become overwhelming. Revised national accounts for 1983 and 1984, which had not been available at the time of the writing of the essay, show that real per capita GDP had declined in every year since 1975, while manufacturing output had contracted at around 20 per cent a year in the 1980s. It will be interesting to see whether the changes made in 1986 will be sufficient to let the economy escape from rationing. The study suggests that this will also require an increased inflow of resources from abroad, which is unlikely to occur on the requisite scale.

Whatever may happen in the particular case of Tanzania, the authors have performed a valuable service by indicating the dangers of even cosmetic systems of price control in peasant economies subject to large external shocks. It is in such economies that price flexibility is particularly required, but also just in these that the temptation to respond to adverse changes by reinforcing price controls is greatest. If such small and vulnerable economies are to liberalize and to remain liberal, attention must be paid to avoiding these errors. Equally, programmes for economic liberalization need to be designed with the greatest care.

NOTES AND REFERENCES

1. *Toward Sustained Development in Sub-Saharan Africa: a Joint Program of Action* (Washington: World Bank, 1984) pp. 34-5.

2. *Ibid.*, Table 1.1.
3. *Ibid.*
4. For an unfavourable view of the typical IMF 'blunt instruments', see G.K. Helleiner, *The IMF and Africa in the 1980s*, Essays in International Finance No. 152 (Princeton, New Jersey: International Finance Section, Department of Economics, Princeton University, 1983) p. 19. On IMF conditionality, see also C. David Finch, 'Adjustment Policies and Conditionality', in John Williamson (ed.), *IMF Conditionality* (Washington: Institute for International Economics, 1983) and Tony Killick 'IMF Stabilisation Programmes', in Killick (ed.), *The Quest for Economic Stabilisation: the IMF and the Third World* (London: Heinemann Educational Books, for the Overseas Development Institute, 1984).
5. See Ernest Stern, 'World Bank Financing of Structural Adjustment' in Williamson (ed.), *op. cit.*, pp. 91-92.
6. *loc. cit.*, Table 5.1.
7. See Killick, 'Kenya 1975-81', in Killick (ed.), *The IMF and Stabilisation: Developing Country Experiences* (London: Heinemann Educational Books, for the Overseas Development Institute, 1984) p.209. See also Killick, 'Kenya, the IMF and the Unsuccessful Quest for Stabilization', in Williamson (ed.), *op. cit.*, p. 408.
8. *Ibid.*, p.409.
9. See Reginald Herbold Green, 'Political-Economic Adjustment and IMF Conditionality: Tanzania, 1974-81', in Williamson (ed.), *op. cit.*, p. 373.

Chapter 1

Kenyan and Tanzanian Economies Compared

THE THESIS of this study is that the effects of trade liberalization can only be understood in relation to the nature and structure of economic organization within a country. In economies which are subject to severely distorting domestic controls on economic activity all piecemeal liberalizations are likely to fail and it is difficult to design a successful sequence of policy measures. It is not the case, as might be supposed, that the more distorted the economy the easier it is to identify policy improvements. This essay is concerned with two African countries which are similar in both economic structure and control regime — Tanzania and Kenya. It will show how the same liberalization measure will lead to radically different consequences in the two countries because of the different methods used in each country to control economic activity.

A brief description of the economic, political and institutional structure of the two countries is necessary before the effects of trade liberalization can be discussed. As can be seen from Table 1.1, both Kenya and Tanzania are essentially rural societies. The rural population is predominantly engaged in peasant agriculture, growing food for domestic consumption and export crops, of which the most important is coffee. The figures on the growth rates of gross domestic product (GDP), for what they are worth, suggest that Kenya has grown rather more rapidly than Tanzania in both the agricultural and non-agricultural sectors. Within agriculture, domestic food production per head has apparently declined in both countries.

Since much of this production is non-marketed, however, its measurement is very suspect. Export crops have been subject to more divergent trends. As shown in Table 1.2 the volume of coffee production, though quite volatile, was in 1983-84

TABLE 1.1

Economic Structure and Performance

	Kenya	*Tanzania*
Population (millions, mid-1982)	18.1	19.8
of which:		
Urban (%)	15.0	13.0
GNP per capita (1982 $US)	390.0	280.0
GDP growth 1970-82 (% pa)	5.5	4.0
Agriculture:		
share in GDP (1982)	33.0	52.0
growth 1970-82 (% pa)	4.1	2.8
food production per capita (1969-71 = 100, 1980-82)	88.0	88.0
food aid 1981/82 (tonnes'000)	115.0	254.0
Export growth 1970-82 (dollar value % pa)	− 3.3	− 5.8
Net inflow public capital 1982 ($US million)	212.0	221.0
Reserves (months of import coverage 1982)	1.4	0.2
Government revenue (% GNP 1981)	23.0	20.0
Government expenditure (% GNP 1981)	28.0	33.0
of which:		
on health and education (%)	29.0	18.0

SOURCE: *World Development Report 1984*, (New York and Oxford: Oxford University Press, for the World Bank, 1984).

some 45 per cent higher than in 1976-77 in Kenya, whereas in Tanzania it was some 5 per cent lower. A similar production pattern was noticeable for the less important export crops in both countries.

In dollar terms, export earnings in both Kenya and Tanzania declined between 1970 and 1982 but particularly rapidly in Tanzania. The annual average percentage decline over the period does, however, conceal a sharp rise in the years 1976-78 when the world price of coffee quadrupled. In the aftermath of this boom both countries, but especially Tanzania, experienced severe foreign exchange crises. During 1982 Tanzania held reserves sufficient for the supply of imports for only six days. This shortage of foreign exchange occurred

TABLE 1.2

Coffee Production and Prices 1975-84

	Production ('000 metric tonnes)		*Price to farmers (shillings per kilo)*	
Year	Kenya	Tanzania	Kenya	Tanzania
1975/76	66.2	55.4	10.7	10.3
1976/77	80.3	48.7	25.3	17.6
1977/78	97.1	51.5	39.8	12.3
1978/79	84.3	51.8	28.2	10.5
1979/80	75.1	47.9	28.4	13.0
1980/81	91.3	67.3	26.3	13.0
1981/82	90.7	63.5	22.6	9.0
1982/83	88.4	53.8	27.8	12.0
1983/84	95.3	53.0	34.9	16.8

SOURCES: *Kenya Statistical Abstract*, *Tanzania Statistical Abstract* (various years) and unpublished government data.

despite very substantial net inflows of foreign aid, which were in excess of $200 million in 1982 for both countries.

In 1981-82 both countries also received food aid; Tanzania had been receiving such aid since the mid-1970s. Dependence upon aid had, by the early 1980s, become so marked in Tanzania that a considerable component of recurrent government expenditure was financed by it. As can be calculated from Table 1.1, only 60 per cent of government expenditure was financed from revenue compared with 82 per cent in Kenya. Both governments were under pressure to reduce expenditure and raise taxes. Within government expenditure, a higher priority was assigned to health and education in Kenya (29 per cent) than in Tanzania (18 per cent).

Politically both governments espouse 'African Socialism' which may be characterized as a high degree of economic interventionism and a one party state. This label does, however, conceal quite substantial differences. Although formally a one party state, in practice Kenya could be more accurately regarded as a non-party state, certainly it was under Kenyatta. Thus, on his death, the Kanu party was so moribund that it was unclear who might be eligible to attend a party conference to ratify the succession. Members of the Kenya parliament spend large sums to win elections and look to their constituents rather than to the party for support.

In contrast, the ruling political party in Tanzania is organized down to the level of the individual household, every ten households having a 'ten-cell-leader' who is a party official with responsibilities and powers of control. Party officials, many of whom reflect former President Nyerere's ideological suspicion of the market as an allocative mechanism, constitute a powerful and influential group and, in addition, have an interest in the preservation of the administered allocative systems in which they participate.

In both countries the Asian communities, which have traditionally dominated trade, are deeply resented by the African population. In Kenya, the African élite which entered politics and the Civil Service after independence in 1963 used the advantages conferred by these positions not only to compete and participate with Asians in commercial ventures but also to take over the large agricultural interests of departing Europeans. Civil servants, for example, were encouraged to own businesses. In Tanzania, by way of contrast, Nyerere forbade civil servants to have other financial interests. Perhaps as a result, anti-Asian and anti-commerce sentiments intermingled in Tanzania and encouraged the suppression of private commerce. Furthermore, the partially-enforced economic controls that were introduced in Tanzania have, to an extent, been evaded by the private sector. Such evasion was perceived by the authorities as anti-state activity. These attitudes of the authorities reinforced attempts to suppress the black market which had emerged in Tanzania as a result of price controls. During 1983 there was a major crackdown against black market 'racketeers' and 'hoarders'; house-to-house searches were made by brigades of Party workers and summary punishments were handed out.

Government attitudes to agriculture also differed sharply, again perhaps as a result of the direct financial interest in agriculture of the Kenyan élite. The price paid for coffee to farmers in Kenya is very much higher than in Tanzania (see Table 1.2) and is one manifestation of this difference. Conversely, in Tanzania the principal interest group to which the government transferred benefits consisted of urban wage earners. Urban wage earners formed a powerful constituency in the party and a potential threat, should their interests be jeopardized. Interviewed on his reasons for resisting pressure from the International Monetary Fund (IMF) for a devaluation in return for a loan, President Nyerere said, 'I can't just sign and have riots in the streets. We say how much will the people take?'.[1]

Thus, despite a common commitment to 'African Socialism' the interests, ideologies and prejudices of the élites in the two countries differed quite substantially as did the need to placate other groups. These distinct political environments gave rise to different regimes of economic controls which in turn contributed to the performance of the two economies.

The following chapter describes the control regime in the two countries prevailing during the period 1975-84, while Chapter 3 explores the micro-economic consequences of these controls for the behaviour of firms, wage earners, the governments and peasants. The macro-economic consequences of this behaviour are also explained in Chapter 3. In Chapters 4 and 5 the theory and experience of piecemeal trade liberalization in economies with differing control regimes are analysed and finally, in Chapter 6 a more viable approach to trade liberalization is expounded.

REFERENCE

1. *The Times*, 24 November 1984, p. 4.

Chapter 2

Structure of Economic Controls in Kenya and Tanzania

WHILE KENYA and Tanzania are often contrasted as examples of a *laissez-faire* society, on the one hand and of a controlled economy, on the other hand, government intervention has been, in fact, pervasive in both countries.

In both countries trade policy has been dominated by the use of quantitative restrictions. In Kenya, reliance on import licensing was already important in the early 1970s when the end of the easy phase of import substitution was reached after a decade of very rapid growth in manufacturing. Producers then lobbied effectively for protection while Kenya's membership of the East African Community ruled out unilateral changes in tariffs. The system of import licensing which developed in the 1970s involved import bans, quotas and 'no objection' certificates (a statement by a local producer that he could not supply a good). The rules governing this system were vague, leaving much to the discretion of civil servants. While the government used import licences both to control total imports and to afford protection to industry, it did not attempt to achieve more specific objectives: the detailed allocation of imports was left to the discretion of officials and, corruption was inevitable. Moreover, Kenya made very little use of exchange rate changes, maintaining a rate of 9.66 Kenyan shillings to Special Drawing Rights (SDRs)[1] from 1975 to 1981, when the shilling was devalued by 22 per cent.

In Tanzania the system of import controls was much more comprehensive and detailed than in Kenya. Import requirements were estimated at the level of individual firms or projects and licences were allocated on the basis of guidelines decided by the Cabinet. Throughout the 1970s imports of capital goods received priority treatment, followed by intermediate goods, while imports of consumption goods were gradually squeezed out. In 1979 capital goods accounted for 47 per cent of imports, intermediate goods (including oil) for 45 per cent and consumer goods for only 8 per cent (50 per cent of which was food). In 1974, Tanzania adopted a 'basic industries strategy' which involved massive investments in capital-intensive and import-competing industries. The implementation of this strategy was, until the early 1980s, considered of overriding importance. (For an excellent discussion of the strategy see Ellen Hanak.[2]) One effect of this strategy was that the agricultural sector was starved of foreign exchange; a further consequence was that imports continued to be used for capital formation long after it became clear that capacity utilization in industry was declining rapidly. In 1982, capacity utilization levels were estimated as 55 per cent for textiles, 36 per cent for shoes, 30 per cent for cement, 47 per cent for iron sheets and 13 per cent for fertilizers.

As in Kenya, the exchange rate was a major instrument of trade policy. The Tanzanian shilling was pegged, first to the US dollar then to the SDR and finally, from 1979, to a basket of currencies of major trading partners. In terms of the SDR the exchange rate varied in the 1970s in a narrow band of 7.1 to 10.8 shillings. During the 1980s there were several devaluations including one of 20 per cent (to 13 Tanzanian shillings to the SDR) in June 1983.

Two points about Tanzanian import controls deserve to be emphasized. First, as export earnings fell the room for maneouvre in allocating imports declined. Between 1980 and 1982, aid tied to projects accounted for almost 40 per cent of total imports while oil imports accounted for about 30 per cent. Second, there was a tendency to allocate foreign exchange within any priority category in proportion to demand. Allocating foreign exchange to all textile factories, for example, rather than to just one of them may well have increased the under-utilization of capacity.

In both countries price controls applied to a very large number of consumer goods. In Kenya, however, controlled prices were either set at market-clearing levels or were not strictly enforced. There was no ideological commitment to price control. The Minister of Finance once openly described the policy as window dressing: 'you have to be seen to be struggling with inflation, otherwise politically you are not credible'.[3] By contrast, in Tanzania the system of price controls took the cost-plus form, firms being allowed a fixed mark-up over total costs. There is a strong political commitment to this system. It is revealing that a long-term government adviser, Reginald Green, saw abolition of price control as giving up an essential element of Tanzania's socialism.[4]

In urban centres, where surveillance was easy, price controls were rigidly enforced. This led to queueing (which took up a significant amount of time for urban workers), to the rise of a black market and to the production of substitutes in the informal sector. The government's campaign against 'racketeers' and the informal sector made evasion of price control very much more difficult during 1983. The distribution of supplies between urban centres and rural regions was basically a political decision, implemented by the Board of Internal Trade which was responsible for delivering supplies to regional centres. Within regions there was, in theory, a system for allocating supplies between villages, but the system amounted, in practice, to a lottery. A village lost its allocation if it did not pick it up (and pay for it in cash) within five days. Quite often a village was not informed in time, did not have the cash ready or was not able to organize transport.[5] If supplies did arrive in a village they were sold at the controlled price in a village store.

Evidence on the extent of rural shortages of consumer goods is presented in Table 2.1, based on a survey of peasant households in four regions conducted by the authors in 1983.

Peasants were asked about the availability of 21 basic commodities; four representative items from the 21 are shown in Table 2.1. For each of these four items, some 90 per cent of households reported that there had been times during the last year when they had wished to buy the item at the official price but had been unable to do so. During the early 1980s, black markets became less effective in allocating supplies in rural areas as private trading was suppressed more vigorously

TABLE 2.1
Rural Purchases in Official and Black Markets

	Official market			*Black market*		
	Lack of access[a] (%)	*Quantity*[b]	*Variability*[c]	*Lack of access*[a] (%)	*Quantity*[b]	*Variability*[c]
Cooking oil (litre)	96	2.6	0.97	87	2.6	0.95
Soap (bar)	95	2.6	1.00	85	3.0	0.98
Sugar (kilo)	96	2.6	0.94	96	3.0	0.96
Cloth (piece)	94	1.9	0.74	89	1.7	0.81

SOURCE: Survey data gathered by the authors in 1983.
[a]Access is measured by the percentage of respondents who replied that during the last year there were times when they wanted to buy the good and it was not available.
[b]Quantity is what was typically bought when a purchase was made.
[c]Variability is the coefficient of variation of the quantity variable across households.

and as rural transport conditions deteriorated. It can be seen from Table 2.1 that the same goods were as scarce on the black market as on the official market, with up to 96 per cent of households reporting that they were unable to make purchases. This was even the case in border areas, where there was an active market in smuggled goods.

The most important aspect of Tanzanian price control is that, because it did not involve formal rationing, markets not only failed to clear but, in addition, an individual's access to consumer goods became a matter of chance. While the survey found the average quantity of goods purchased to be small, there were very wide variations around the average. For example, though the average purchase of sugar on the black market was only three kilogrammes, 15 per cent of purchases were of nine kilogrammes or more. A common measure of differences from the average, the coefficient of variation, is shown in Table 2.1 and confirms that for all four goods on both official and black markets the quantity available varied considerably between purchases. As will be argued later, the monetary consequences of this seriously hamper any attempt at liberalization.

Two political constraints underlay this system. First, there was the government's commitment to price control itself. Secondly, while the government (through the Board of Internal Trade) was able to change the allocation of supplies both between town and rural areas and between rural regions, any increase in the rural share was politically difficult as long as this could be achieved only at the expense of the real incomes of urban workers.

Intervention in markets for food grains took a similar form in both countries, differing only in extent. Consumer and producer prices were set by the government, and inter-district trade was the legal monopoly of a state marketing board. Government price intervention favoured consumers at the expense of producers. Perhaps because of the greater political influence of urban wage earners, food prices in Tanzania were more depressed by these controls than in Kenya. When 1960 is used as the base year, it can be shown that producer prices had fallen in real terms by 42 per cent in Tanzania by 1980 but by only 26 per cent in Kenya. In both countries the legal monopoly of the marketing board was widely evaded through extensive 'parallel' markets. In Tanzania, however, these markets were highly fragmented because of the greater severity of enforcement and the collapse of the rural transport network. Prices varied widely over time and between locations in Tanzania, and availability of goods was spasmodic.

The difficulties of conducting trade with inadequate transport overwhelmed the Tanzanian National Milling Corporation (NMC) which made no attempt to sell food in rural areas except in cases of famine. It thus defaulted on its legal obligation to provide a national marketing system; it has instead, confined itself to the role of urban food supplier. Worse still, the NMC has been unable to purchase enough food domestically, to meet even urban demand. The causes of this failure go beyond the decline in the producer price. To feed the urban population, therefore, the government resorted to food imports, mostly financed through aid. The imported food was then sold by the government to the NMC, which in turn sold it to urban consumers. Thus the NMC was more like an import agency than a crop marketing authority. In the short run the government benefited by the addition to its revenues, though in the long run it incurred avoidable foreign exchange liabilities. Moreover, even with imports there was insufficient food available at official prices to feed the urban population. Around one third of urban consumption was met from the fragmented parallel markets and from food grown by urban households.

In Kenya, the market was geographically segmented by the prohibition on private inter-district trade, but there was normally sufficient supply for the state marketing board to meet urban requirements.

Export crops in both countries have generally been marketed internationally through government monopolies. In Tanzania these monopolies extended through the domestic economy and included control over deliveries of inputs as well as over the purchase of output. Coffee, the major export crop was, on occasion, subject to high explicit rates of tax, but many crops were subject to rising implicit taxes in the form of increasing rates of deductions charged by the marketing authorities. This probably reflects the fact that monopolists had little need to resist pressures for cost increases.[6] The domestic price of export crops was not closely related to world prices. Prices were set by the Cabinet and based on the recommendations of the Marketing Development Bureau. The latter was concerned to equalize the return to a day's labour on different crops, both export and domestic food crops. Thus, crop prices reflected costs; this is analogous to the industrial cost-plus price control system. In Kenya, the major crop authorities had a more limited role, marketing at the local level having elements of competition through politically powerful marketing cooperatives. No significant export taxes were levied and marketing margins were both significantly lower than in Tanzania and displayed no trend. Domestic prices broadly reflected world prices. Hence, although the formal apparatus of public marketing was not dissimilar, the use of these controls differed markedly.

Both countries offer examples of financial repression. In Kenya nominal interest rates were typically kept constant for years until 1980; the rate for Post Office Savings Bank deposits was set at 5 per cent in 1975, where it remained until 1980. This meant that all deposit rates were strongly negative in real terms. The flow of credit to the agricultural sector was minute, amounting to less than 3 per cent of the value of output. Rural credit was rationed *intensively*, access to it being restricted to farmers with large holdings, to those who grew particular crops or to farmers with relatively stable, non-agricultural sources of income.[7]

In Tanzania the financial system consisted entirely of public institutions. These played an accommodating role; most financial flows occurred *within* the public sector. The profits of industrial parastatals, for example, were deposited with the National Bank of Commerce and were then used to extend seasonal credit to crop parastatals, their direction and magnitude was often determined by non-financial government policies. There was little scope for independent financial intermediaries. The sectoral direction of credit was laid down in the Annual Finance and Credit Plan. Rural credit was dominated by lending to villages (which in 1980-81 accounted for 90 per cent of the loans of the Tanzania Rural Development Bank [TRDB]) and was largely tied to the provision of seasonal inputs under externally financed projects. Unlike Kenya, credit rationing took an *extensive* form — all peasants received less than they would like to borrow, and credit was largely limited to short-term loans.

The villages, the crop authorities and TRDB all play a role in loan collection and institutional confusion was partly responsible for the increasing severity of credit rationing: as the rates of loan recovery declined, lending was further restricted. The Tanzanian peasant had no access to an attractive financial asset: deposits in the Post Office Savings Bank were unattractive both because of the travel time which would be involved in making deposits or withdrawals and because of the low yields offered.

In both countries the large share of the public sector in capital formation (about 50 per cent at the end of the 1970s), offered the government an instrument for controlling the direction of investment directly. The countries differed in the use made of this instrument. In Kenya slightly more than one per cent of public investment went to manufacturing in the late 1970s. In Tanzania the share of industry soared from one per cent in the second to the 23 per cent projected for the third five-year plan (1976 to 1981). Whatever its merits in the long run, the industrial investment programme made the foreign exchange crisis very much worse in the short run.

Tanzania invested in some activities which were likely to be net users of foreign exchange in the best of circumstances (cashew processing, for example, in which value added was negative at world prices). Investment in other activities such as textiles could be perfectly efficient in the absence of rationing. The problem was that the combination of the sheer size of the investment programme and the item-specific extensive rationing of imports turned even firms which were potentially efficient into net users of foreign exchange. There was a vicious circle: exports fell as the supply of agricultural inputs and consumer goods to the rural sector declined. As long as the government continued to react to the declining availability of foreign exchange by approving a smaller fraction of the applications for imports of *all* firms the efficiency of the use of foreign exchange was likely to continue to decline. The political cost of any switch to intensive rationing would have been high, however, because it would have involved shutting down some newly-built plants, at least temporarily.

NOTES AND REFERENCES

1. The SDR is a weighted average of major currencies determined by the IMF.
2. Ellen E. Hanak, 'The Tanzanian Balance of Payments Crisis: Causes, Consequences and Lessons for a Survival Strategy' MA Thesis, University of Dar es Salaam, 1981.
3. Kenya Association of Manufacturers, *East Africa Report on Finance and Industry*, Nairobi, June 1977, p. 12.
4. See R.H. Green, 'Industrialization in Tanzania' in M. Fransman (ed.), *Industry and Accumulation in Africa* (London: Heinemann, 1981) p. 90.
5. See S. Shepherd, 'Marketing of Agricultural and Other Commodities in the Mbeya Region', a Report for the Food and Agriculture Organization, Dar es Salaam, 1982, p. 138.
6. See Matthew Guerreiro, 'The Structure and Performance of Agricultural Marketing in Kenya and Tanzania', M Litt Thesis, University of Oxford, 1984.
7. See J.D. von Pischke, 'The Political Economy of Farm Credit in Kenya', PhD Thesis, University of Glasgow, 1977.

Chapter 3

Sectoral Effects of Economic Controls

HOW DID the various controls alter the behaviour of the major types of agent in the two East African economies, namely, firms, urban wage earners, black marketeers, governments and, most importantly, peasant households (who comprised some 80 per cent of the entire population)? In each case we find that the control regime can alter behaviour radically, producing paradoxical responses to policy instruments.

The Effect on Firms

It is often convenient to distinguish between public and private enterprises since they may differ systematically in the nature of their objectives and in the constraints they face. These differences concern the degree of profit motivation, the extent of financial discipline and the related capacity to sustain losses, the incentives to productive and organizational efficiency and the scale of interference in the distribution and use of profits. In the present analysis there is an additional reason for making this distinction: the two categories of enterprise may behave differently when faced with rationing, a possibility that must be explored.

An enterprise of either type obtains revenue from selling its output while purchasing material inputs, paying for labour and servicing its debts. Since these expenses pre-date revenue, the enterprise requires a stock of working financial capital. Under conditions of rationing the enterprise is able to sell all its output (and it could sell more) at the going price. It is unable to obtain all the input materials that it requires, however, because there is excess demand for both intermediate as well as final products. What happens when the enterprise moves into such a regime from a previously unrationed state?

At first the enterprise's money holdings will rise. This is because its outgoings are curtailed (its purchases of inputs are rationed) but, initially, its receipts are not. Since the input-constrained enterprise will always choose to use available inputs in production, it will not be able to vary production independently in order to build up or run down money holdings.

When money holdings depart from their desired level, however, privately-owned enterprises face a portfolio balance problem (that is, how to redistribute their wealth). The onset of rationing has had three effects on the owners' wealth. First, it has altered the equity valuation of the firm. The fall in volume of production and therefore sales will tend to lower the equity value, but if the firm is able to exploit the shortages by raising its prices the value will rise. In the latter circumstance, the firm's net cash flow will also have risen. Second, the level of desired working balances will have fallen because of the reduced availability of inputs. Since firms have access to credit, unlike peasants, they do not need to accumulate precautionary balances. Thirdly, rationing of consumer goods is likely to reduce the proportion of the owner's wealth he chooses to hold in cash as opposed to other assets.

It is not possible for owners, taken as a group, to run down their excess money balances by purchase of goods, because these are rationed. As there is no bond market, the two alternative portfolio or wealth-holding adjustments are acquisition of property and acquisition of foreign exchange, which differ in their impact. Since property is in fixed supply, attempts to purchase it do not create fresh income or production flows. They merely yield capital gains to those who own the property. In a society in which peasants own the bulk of property, there would be a transfer of purchasing power to them, but where they do not, the price of privately held property must be bid up to the point at which the cash and property components of the portfolios of the wealthy are again in balance. In effect, the wealthy try to reduce their cash holdings by purchasing property. Since they must buy it from other wealthy individuals, the collective holdings of cash and property are not altered by these purchases. The process will only stop when the price of property is high enough to deter further purchases. Thus the initial disequilibrium is equilibrated simply by price changes since real adjustments are impossible.

The alternative mechanism involves real leakage of the excess purchasing power. In the quantity-constrained circumstances under consideration, the only means of achieving such a leakage is by exchanging domestic currency for foreign currency, either to obtain goods or to diversify the portfolio into foreign assets. Since foreign exchange is rationed, this cannot be achieved legally. Devices for achieving it illegally are black market currency dealings, smuggling of goods and over-invoicing of imports. The consequences of each are likely to be similar and over-invoicing is used as an illustration in the following example.

When inputs are rationed, they carry an economic rent — that is, they are worth more than their face value. This rent may accrue to final consumers as consumer surplus, if they receive rationed supplies of the final good at a price below what they are prepared to pay. Alternatively, part or all of it may be appropriated at an earlier stage either by the firm itself or by black marketeers. For the firm there are two possibilities, depending on whether it is free to set its output price or not.

If the firm is able to raise its output price to exploit the shortages, then it can appropriate the rent directly. For a given allocation of foreign exchange, the owner of the firm would have to decide whether to extract this rent entirely in profits in domestic currency or to take it partly in the form of foreign currency. If his imported inputs are correctly invoiced, he maximizes the volume of imports and hence domestic sales of the firm; the excess returns due to rationing accrue entirely in domestic currency. On the other hand, if he colludes with his supplier to give an inflated price on the invoice, fewer goods will be imported and the volume of domestic sales will be reduced. If demand is reasonably elastic, his domestic currency profits will fall, but he will also obtain a foreign currency holding equal to his share of the amount of the over-invoicing.

If the firm's output price is controlled by the government, as was typical in Tanzania, it might appear that the firm is unable to obtain a share of these rents. We have noted earlier, however, that the type of price control used in Tanzania involved a mark-up on costs. Under this regime the firm's owner has two incentives to inflate his import costs: it increases his domestic currency profit on a given volume of sales, and it gives him an illicit foreign currency gain as well. Indeed, with this type of price control and rationing of both inputs and outputs the only way to increase domestic profits is by inflating costs, so there would be an incentive to over-invoice even if the portfolio balance argument did not apply. The analysis of the preceding paragraphs presupposes that import rationing is by value. If it is by volume instead these adverse effects will be exacerbated.

The firm which is subject to price controls will be able to capture only a fraction of the economic rent directly. A part may remain with consumers in the form of consumer surplus: that is, consumers would have been prepared to pay more for their purchases of the good than the controlled price they paid. Another part will accrue to black-marketeers who obtain privileged access to supplies at controlled prices.

In any event, such behaviour — the inflation of import costs — is likely to become more attractive the larger the excess supply of domestic currency in the hands of the wealthy traders. The tendency towards such behaviour will be exacerbated if rationing becomes tighter, since the share of rents in total revenue will tend to increase while holdings of domestic money becomes less attractive. Over-invoicing is also a very damaging type of behaviour, since it has consequences similar to a deterioration in the barter terms of trade.

Now contrast the behaviour of a public enterprise. It is true that corrupt officials might also practice over-invoicing, but for the enterprise as a whole the portfolio balance problem does not arise. The emergence of excess money holdings may be prevented by holding output constant, giving rise to black market behaviour. Alternatively, excess returns may be dissipated by increasing employment, that is by purchasing labour services which are not needed. Under a cost-plus pricing regime, coupled with excess demand for the products of the enterprise, there are no financial penalties associated with this type of behaviour; on the contrary it will enhance profits. There is also pressure for employment creation. Workers are anxious to obtain employment for relatives, managers obtain prestige thereby and the government hopes to reduce urban social pressures in this way. Since the output of the enterprise is constrained by its rationed supply of intermediate inputs, the additional workers produce no additional output. Hence the extra purchasing power placed in their hands simply serves to increase excess demand for consumer goods.

To summarize: both types of enterprise are encouraged to inflate costs, but there is a special incentive to inflate the import component in the private case, and the domestic component in the public case.

The position in the Kenyan economy was somewhat different. An over-valued exchange rate coupled with foreign exchange rationing may still make over-invoicing attractive as a mechanism for portfolio adjustment. Firms are free to raise domestic output prices, however, and so over-invoicing is reduced to a decision as to where to realize rents rather than a necessary condition for realizing them.

Urban Wage Earners and Black Marketeers

Whereas in Kenya successful peasants and business owners formed powerful political interest groups, in Tanzania the maintenance of the living standards of urban wage earners was probably the dominant political constraint facing the government. Instances of the government's concern to placate urban wage earners were the cheap food grain policy already described (Chapter 2) and the reluctance to lay off workers despite excess capacity caused by shortages of imported inputs. Above all, the need to conciliate urban workers probably motivated the attempt to control the prices of consumer goods at a level that produced scarcities. Scarcity was so pronounced that urban workers could not spend all their wages on goods bought at official prices. As a result an urban black market developed in these goods, together with an informal sector producing services (such as spare parts of inferior quality) for which there would have been no market, were goods unrationed. Entrepreneurs in the black market acquired goods at official prices, sold some of them at black market prices and used the profits to finance their own consumption. Supplies were diverted into the black market at all stages from the unloading of imports to retail distribution. Some managers of firms producing goods locally were large-scale 'racketeers', buying-up the production of their firms at official prices and re-selling it. Small-scale operators in the black market were to be found outside shops waiting for the opportunity to buy goods for resale should the shop receive a delivery. If black marketeers and informal sector producers had spent all their profits on consumer goods and the output of the informal sector then black market prices would have risen explosively. As prices rose so would profit margins also and this would have enabled black marketeers to retain more goods for their own consumption, thereby exacerbating scarcity and driving prices higher.

The existence of the informal sector, while having distributional consequences, does not affect this analysis since expenditure on its services generates incomes which in turn become demand for goods. Thus, expenditure on the informal sector does not constitute a leakage that reduces excess demand. The black market is stable only if black marketeers choose to hoard some of their profits in financial assets. In Tanzania, as already discussed, there were only two financial assets, domestic currency (which it was risky to hold in large quantities) and illegally-acquired foreign exchange. As with firms, black marketeers faced a portfolio balance problem and it seems likely that a considerable amount of foreign exchange was lost to the government through the acquisition of foreign assets by black marketeers. For a quantification of over-invoicing see Chapter 7 of David Bevan *et al*, 1986.[1]

The interactions between wages, the availability of goods and black market prices generate curious and powerful macro-economic paradoxes. The existence of the urban black market means that wage earners face two sets of prices, some purchases being made at official prices (which are recorded in the price index) and some at black market prices (which are generally excluded from the index). For a given aggregate availability of goods, an increase in money wages will increase the excess of desired expenditure over the value of available goods at official prices and hence drive up prices in the black market. This will widen profit margins for black marketeers, thereby increasing their income and consumption. Given the total availability of goods intended for wage earners (a proportion of which is diverted to the consumption of black marketeers), an increase in the consumption of black marketeers implies a reduction in the consumption of wage earners. Hence, for a given aggregate availability of goods and a given level of controlled prices, an increase in wages reduces the living standards of wage earners.

To extend the argument, even if the wage increase was combined with an increase in the quantity of goods intended for wage earners it is quite possible for the living standards of wage earners to fall as a result. This implies that satisfying the political constraint that the living standards of urban workers be maintained is not a simple matter of matching wages to the official price index. More appropriately, an index is required which measures both official and black market prices and also the proportion of transactions on each market.

THE INFLUENCE OF GOVERNMENT

Governments can set tax rates, but total tax revenue, and hence the size of the budget deficit, will depend on the behaviour of private economic agents. Budget deficits may be financed by money creation, or by borrowing at home or abroad. In Kenya and Tanzania, the scope for domestic borrowing has been very limited, and the scope for discretionary variation in it more or less negligible, because the bulk of domestic borrowing arises from the portfolio requirements of provident funds and the like which are legally restricted to holding only government-issued assets. It is assumed that foreign borrowing is also fixed so that residual financing must come from money creation.

If prices are flexible, the government is able to alter the nominal stock of money, and if the nominal stock diverges from that required to give the desired volume of real balances at the initial price level, prices will adjust accordingly. When a government succeeds in controlling prices, changes in the nominal money stock necessarily involve equivalent changes in the real money stock. Except temporarily, during an adjustment to a shock, the government is unable to induce the private sector to hold excess real money balances. Peasants can simply cut back on the production for markets, so lowering their money holdings. Enterprises will not adjust their production but will adjust their money holdings by over-invoicing or employment expansion. The only mechanism of those previously discussed that would allow the government to alter equilibrium real balances within a given regime of commodity rationing and price controls is that of inflation in property prices. Leaving this mechanism aside, the level of the money stock becomes endogenous.

A way of summarizing this argument is to say that imposition of price controls requires a government to exercise greater fiscal discipline. Given the restrictions on borrowing, the path of government expenditure and that of tax revenue must be consistent with a growth of the money stock that the country's citizens are prepared to hold at the controlled prices.

The Supply Response of Peasants

The control regimes in which Kenyan and Tanzanian peasants operated, although similar in respect of the crops they sold, differed in relation to the ability of the rural population to purchase consumer goods. Whereas consumer goods were readily available in rural areas in Kenya, in Tanzania they were subject to severe shortages whether purchased at official prices or on the repressed and highly fragmented rural black market. Our major thesis is that peasant supply response changes radically and becomes perverse once the consumer goods market is heavily controlled.

In Tanzania the onset of consumer goods shortages dates from the late-1970s, a period too brief for statistical tests of supply response. In a study by staff of the IMF, however, that dealt with supply responses to price changes over the longer period of 1972 to 1981, marked differences were found between Kenya and Tanzania.[2] Whereas in Kenya a change in crop price was found to produce a statistically significant and substantial change in agricultural output, in Tanzania, the response to price changes was negligible and statistically insignificant. The explanation for this may lie no further than in the poor quality of agricultural data. However, the apparent absence of response to price changes in Tanzania over the period 1972 to 1981 is consistent with the thesis that there was a switch from a positive response in the early 1970s to a perverse response from the late-1970s.

For the following analysis peasants are characterized as producing food and cash crops (which may be thought of as coffee) and consuming goods, food and leisure. Peasants are, however, assumed to produce food for their own consumption only, since as was explained in Chapter 2, there was no rural maize market on which they could rely. In these circumstances nothing is lost by neglecting the choice between leisure and work on food production; thus, the following analysis focusses on the choice between time spent on leisure and food combined (described as 'leisure') and time spent on coffee production.

Consider first, the simple case of a barter economy in which coffee is exchanged directly for consumer goods. In the absence of price controls consumer goods will not be rationed and peasants will optimize by choosing to work on producing coffee up to the point at which the disutility of the last hour of work equals the utility derived from the goods purchased with that work. Once control-induced shortages are introduced, however, the peasant cannot purchase all the goods he wishes to buy. The effects of a rural black market are abstracted from in the present analysis. (In David Bevan *et al* (1986) it is indicated that similar, though more complex, conclusions concerning supply response follow once such a market is included.) The peasant will, therefore, choose to do only enough work on coffee to pay for the goods which he expects to be available, since further coffee production would be wasted effort, yielding no additional consumption. In this situation, an increase in the barter price of coffee will reduce coffee output, unless it coincides with a changed expectation of the availability of consumer goods. With a constant expectation of availability of goods to purchase (and hence of expenditure), the peasant will wish to maintain his coffee income constant. An increase in the price of coffee will then induce an equal proportionate reduction in supply. (In other words, the supply elasticity is minus unity.) While supply response to price is perverse, an increase in the availability of consumer goods at a given coffee price will induce a corresponding increase in coffee production, since peasants wish to buy more goods in exchange for coffee than is possible at prevailing prices.

This simple analysis of perverse response to price and positive response to increased availability of the goods peasants wish to purchase is complicated once we move from a barter economy to one in which goods can be purchased only for money. Peasants in Tanzania no longer had significant opportunities to barter and, given that their transactions involved money, their supply response to changes in both prices and availability of goods may have been perverse.

Liberalization is then fraught with difficulties: even though in an undistorted economy the coffee price would be higher (relative to the price of goods) and goods would be readily available, attempts to move directly towards this equilibrium are likely to make things worse. It is important, therefore, to understand how such perverse responses may come about.

Suppose that peasants receive cash from their coffee sales at the close of the harvest, consume goods evenly through the year, and hold money balances only to finance their annual consumption. When goods are unrationed, therefore, the maximum money stock held by the peasant (which he holds just after being paid for his coffee) is equal to his planned annual expenditure. When the availability of goods is limited, the money stock that the peasant chooses to hold depends critically upon the form of rationing.

When there is a known ration, as was the case in wartime Britain, future expenditure is also known, so the desired maximum money stock is equal to this (reduced) annual expenditure. In Tanzania, however, as in many present-day price control systems, availability of rationed goods was a matter of chance. Although shortage was the norm, a household might have had the opportunity of purchasing increased supplies of the rationed goods in which event its ability to purchase was determined by the money held. This has important consequences for the relation between availability of goods and money holdings. If the household knew for certain the amount of goods that would be available money holdings would be proportional. Since the household cannot buy as much as it wants it will always want to hold just enough money to buy the maximum amount available, hence money stocks will decline if rationing becomes more severe. If availability is uncertain, however, there is a second effect working in the opposite direction. If the household were to hold a money stock sufficient to buy the average quantity available it would not be able to profit from above-average availability for lack of money. Hence it will want to hold more money to reduce the probability of being so constrained. The strength of this second effect depends on the utility of leisure (since money can be accumulated only by working more), on the expected variability of the availability of goods to purchase and on the household's aversion to risk. If this second effect is strong enough, then the optimal money stock will first rise and then falls as availability of consumer goods decreases. The analysis is illustrated in Appendix I.

Changes in money holdings matter because they imply changes in coffee output. If the peasant chooses to increase his money stock then he is choosing to produce more coffee than is required to finance his expected expenditure on goods. Conversely, a reduction in holdings of money can only be effected by producing less coffee than would be required to cover expenditure. The effects of a change in goods availability on coffee output must therefore be separated into two time periods: the short-run response during which peasants are adjusting their money stocks to the new desired level, and the long run response which remains once money holdings are fully adjusted. The short- and long-run responses may either reinforce or offset each other.

If the availability of goods to purchase deteriorates so that coffee output is reduced in the long run, this is at least partly offset in the short-run by peasants producing more coffee in order to accumulate money balances. Coffee production may therefore be not much altered in the short run, as availability of goods deteriorates. Further deterioration in the availability of goods, however, induces a reduction in money stocks so that the long run reduction in coffee production is more pronounced than in the short run.

Conversely, if they start with restricted availability of consumer goods but full availability is then restored, peasants find themselves with a windfall of excess money balances to be spent. If they discount future consumption at a high rate this excess money will be spent rapidly, partly by consuming more goods and partly by doing less work on coffee production. Thus, the short-run effect of an improvement in the availability of goods can be a reduction in coffee production.

So far the discussion has focussed upon the coffee output of the peasant as determined by an unexplained level of availability of goods. Now allow for the fact that, in aggregate, cash crop production, being virtually Tanzania's entire exports, determined foreign exchange earnings and hence the ability to import both consumer goods and the inputs needed to produce consumer goods locally. Given the price controls, the availability of consumer goods is then indirectly determined by the level of cash crop production as well as directly determining it. A reduction in coffee production will worsen availability of goods to purchase, which will, in turn, further reduce coffee production.

If the government's objective is to maximize the quantity of imported goods available to the urban sector it must exploit its monopoly power as the sole marketing agent for coffee by setting the domestic price below the world price. Given the relationship between rural availability of imports and coffee production the government maximizes its revenue by setting the producer price of coffee so that the marginal rate at which peasants 'transform' the imports made available to them into coffee is equal to the world price. This drives a wedge between the domestic and world price of coffee that is equivalent to an 'optimum' tariff.

Once price control is combined with a given urban claim on imports, a claim which represents political constraints on the government and as such makes certain public expenditures sacrosanct, peasants may become subject to rationing and the economy will acquire an implosive feature. A shortfall in production of export crops may, because of the urban claim on imports, reduce the availability of goods to peasants below what they expected to receive. If they do not consider this reduction to be transient, they will plan to produce less coffee in future and the economy will contract even further in the next period. The introduction of rationing into the peasant sector also implies that it can no longer be decided unambiguously whether the producer price is too high or too low. The price may be too high in the sense that, for given rural availability of imported consumer goods, peasants would produce more if the price were lowered. At the same time, the producer price may be too low in the sense that it would have to be increased (along with the rural availability) if the 'optimum' is to be reached. These ideas are illustrated geometrically in Appendix II.

So far, the possibility of a cumulative contraction in coffee output in conditions of certainty has been discussed implicitly. When rationing is a matter of chance, our earlier discussion on optimum money holdings suggests that the process of implosion can be divided into two phases. In the first phase, as availability of goods for peasants to purchase deteriorates, desired money holdings rise and peasants temporarily produce more coffee than when their money stocks were at their chosen levels. Consequently, even though the rationing point represents an unstable equilibrium the decline in output will be dampened initially. Once availability deteriorates, however, to the point at which peasants choose to reduce their money stocks, the long-run tendency to implosive output reductions is accelerated by short-run dishoarding of money. Hence, once a price controlled economy stumbles into a regime of shortages which peasants expect to be sustained, output is subject to initially creeping, but eventually rapid, cumulative decline.

Now consider how credit controls affect investment decisions. In Chapter 2 it was suggested that both the Kenyan and Tanzanian economies were characterized by financial repression. Interest rate ceilings lower the total volume of savings (and hence investment) and change the composition of investment thereby, as rationed credit is allocated to low-risk proposals. Peasant agriculture is likely to be disadvantaged in its access to formal credit sources. In East Africa this was particularly serious because of the virtual absence of an informal credit market.

A survey of Kenyan peasants by the authors in 1982 found that only 2 per cent of households had had any interest-bearing credit transactions with other households (either as lenders or borrowers) in that year. The curtailment of access to credit has most probably reduced agricultural investment. Thus, in Kenya, in the three major types of investment, coffee planting, purchase of livestock, and purchase of land, only 2 per cent of households had financed any investment in those three categories by loans over the period 1975-82. Furthermore, the means by which investments had been financed suggested that many households faced cash constraints; nearly half of the investments had been met out of non-farm income or asset disposals, neither of which are available to most peasant households. In Tanzania, access by peasants to credit was even more severely curtailed than in Kenya, but it is clear that the relaxation of this constraint alone would not have raised agricultural investment. While consumer goods were in limited supply there was no incentive to raise agricultural output. Hence, liberalization of these two similar financial regimes would have yielded dissimilar effects.

NOTES AND REFERENCES

1. D. Bevan, P. Collier, J.W. Gunning, A. Bigsten, P. Horsnell, *Trade Shocks in Controlled Economies* (Washington: World Bank, 1986).
2. See Marian E. Bond, 'Agricultural Responses to Prices in Sub-Saharan African Countries', *IMF Staff Papers* Volume XXX, December, 1983, pp. 703-26. Note that the elasticities reported by Bond in Tables 4 and 5 are not consistent and correspondence with her has established that Table 5 should be ignored.

Chapter 4

Alternative Instruments of Liberalization

THE PRECEDING discussion has suggested that once a controlled economy has entered a regime of rationing, trade liberalization may be very difficult to achieve. In this chapter the consequences of each of four common liberalization policies in rationed and unrationed regimes respectively are examined. The policies are: (i) an increase in producer prices for cash crops, (ii) an increase in the domestic price of imports (consumer prices), (iii) devaluation and (iv) a temporary improvement in import availability (an extra inflow of aid, for example). These policies were, indeed, either implemented or actively considered in Kenya and Tanzania during the period under consideration, and the problems actually encountered are therefore discussed.

Increases in Producer Prices

Since both Kenya and Tanzania are small producers, the dollar prices of both export crops and imported food crops are effectively fixed. What the government can alter are the domestic currency prices of these crops relative to the domestic currency price of consumer goods. In the normal case, typified by Kenya, where consumer goods are unrationed, a positive supply response to a rise in producer prices would be expected and indeed, occurred. This increase in the supply of crops is then translated into an increased supply of consumer goods via the current account of the balance of payments. Peasants will have an increased demand for these goods, of course, so the supply available to the rest of the economy after providing for the demand of the rural communities may still fall. It is quite possible in Kenya (and more likely in Tanzania) that by the early 1980s the domestic coffee price was below the 'optimum' level (that is steeper than the ray OB in the figure in Appendix II). Hence, it can be said that, in the case of an unrationed goods market the coffee price should be raised.

By contrast, if the goods market is rationed, as it was in Tanzania, raising the coffee price will generate a perverse supply response for the reasons outlined in Chapter 3. There is a paradox: although the coffee price may be too low, to raise it, would worsen the situation. This naturally suggests that lowering the coffee price might improve the situation. This alternative is investigated through a second popular policy recommendation, namely an increase in the price of consumer goods.

Increases in Consumer Prices

In Tanzania, an increase in the price of consumer goods might have been brought about either by converting import quotas into tariffs or by the Price Commission's granting a higher mark-up over costs. The former would have raised government revenue; the latter, corporate profits. In either case the increase in prices would have had effects on the urban economy, real money balances and the terms of trade facing peasants.

Consider, first, the urban economy. As discussed in Chapter 3, in a regime in which most goods are rationed (a rationed economy), an increase in official prices or the equivalent — a reduction in money wages — would have reduced the incomes of black marketeers and thereby tended to raise the living standards of urban wage earners. Clearly not all wage earners would have benefited; those who made a relatively large proportion of their purchases at official prices would have suffered. Hence, a price increase would have redistributed welfare among urban groups but would not have reduced total urban consumption, unless the price increases were so considerable as to eliminate shortages altogether. Thus, if part of the objective is to release imports for other uses, the price increase would have to be very large — a situation quite different from that in an economy where goods are unrationed (an unrationed economy) such as in Kenya.

Now consider the effect on peasants of a price increase. This has two elements: a reduction in real cash balances and a decline in the relative price of coffee. The former unambiguously raises coffee production as peasants attempt to restore their real cash balances. From the earlier discussion it might appear that in a rationed economy a fall in the relative price of coffee would also raise coffee production. It is indeed the case that a marginal reduction in the coffee price would generally raise output but a large reduction would reduce it. There is a critical coffee price below which insufficient quantities of coffee are produced to satisfy the demands of urban wage earners for consumer goods. If the price should fall below the critical level then the economy would collapse implosively back into rationing. (A discussion of this process is given in Appendix II.) When the critical coffee price is not known any significant reduction in its price relative to the price of consumer goods could be extremely destabilizing. In Tanzania, in the period 1975-84, the domestic price of coffee might well have been below the critical level.

Suppose that the price of coffee were raised in line with the increase in consumer prices. This policy 'package' in fact amounts to a devaluation.

Devaluation of the Currency

A devaluation raises the domestic currency price of both imported consumer goods and of export crops by the same percentage. It therefore differs from an increase in consumer prices by avoiding a deterioration in the relative price of coffee. In either a rationed or an unrationed economy a devaluation would unambiguously raise coffee production in the short-term, while peasants restore their real cash balances. In a rationed economy, if this temporary increase in coffee output were sufficient to carry the economy out of the rationing regime there would then be a permanent increase in the production of coffee as the economy would generate a self-sustaining expansion to the unrationed equilibrium. If the temporary increase in output were insufficient to escape the rationing regime, output would fall again once money balances had been restored. The phase of accelerating implosion would then only have been postponed.

A devaluation which enabled the economy to escape from rationing could ultimately raise the real living standards of all urban wage earners through improved availability of goods, even with constant money wages. Initially, however, the redistributions among urban workers might make a devaluation politically difficult. Until black market prices fell (as they would if availability of goods to urban areas were maintained at a constant level), all wage earners would experience reduced standards of living. This fear of a genuinely difficult very short-run is a political obstacle to a devaluation of the magnitude required to escape rationing.

In an unrationed regime such as in Kenya a devaluation with constant money wages would secure a cut in real wages and urban consumption of imports, not merely an increase in official prices offset by a decrease in black market prices. In the absence of rationing in commodity and labour markets, producers would increase production in response to a real wage cut. This familiar argument in favour of a devaluation did not apply in Tanzania. Since production is constrained by imports, real wage cuts have no output effect. Devaluation is, therefore, less effective as a device for improving the balance of payments in a rationed regime.

Temporary Increase in Consumer Goods Imports

The final piecemeal policy change to be considered is that of a temporary increase in the availability of consumer goods secured by an increase in imports of final or intermediate goods. Such a policy is only of relevance in a rationed economy. It could be achieved either by an increase in foreign aid or by a diversion of existing aid and government-owned foreign exchange from investment. During the period considered, the latter would have had few short-run consequences for output, since a shortage of imported intermediate inputs constrained output at a level at which there was considerable excess capacity.

In a barter economy a temporary increase in availability of modest proportions would often be sufficient to restore the unrationed equilibrium. In a monetary economy, however, extra import requirements are very much larger. By 1984 real money balances in Tanzania were double the level which would have been chosen in an unrationed equilibrium. An improvement in the availability of goods would have caused these balances to be run down, thereby temporarily increasing imports. But a halving of money balances would have required around $US600 million of extra imports, an aid inflow of quite unrealistic magnitude. Further, depending upon the rate at which peasants discount the future, it has been shown that it is quite possible for improved availability to induce a short-run reduction in coffee production. Thus a generous aid donor financing a large-scale rescue operation may face the unnerving short-term responses of soaring imports and falling exports.

Chapter 5

How Liberalization has Worked in Practice

WHAT WAS the experience of Kenya and Tanzania in attempting to implement the various policies so far considered? Both the impetus for, and the problems encountered by, their attempts at trade liberalization resulted from shocks in world trade. The two countries experienced four violent shocks in world prices in less than a decade: the oil price increase of 1974, the huge increase in coffee and tea prices in 1976 and 1977, the subsequent sharp fall in these prices and, finally, the second oil price shock in 1979-80.

The marked changes of fortune had three types of effect on each country. First, the volatility in government revenue destabilized government expenditure. Second, both in periods of severe balance of payments deficit and of strong surplus attempts at trade liberalization were encouraged. In the former case, the power of the International Monetary Fund (IMF) was increased and in the latter case trade liberalization was part of the government response to a relaxation of constraints upon it. Third, trade shocks interacted with the system of controls to produce either changes in the price level, as in Kenya, or compounded domestic policy errors as in Tanzania.

In Kenya, the period after the coffee boom was marked by a loss of control (particularly of public expenditure) but not, at least initially, by changes in the system of control. Kenya adjusted in part by borrowing from external sources and, in part by squeezing imports. The volume of imports fell by 25 per cent between 1975 and 1981 and the increased severity of the rationing of raw materials contributed to growing excess capacity in manufacturing. By making Kenya more dependent upon IMF and World Bank financing at a time when both agencies were insisting on the removal of quantitative restrictions on trade, the trade shocks contributed to a change in trade policy. The 1980 Budget speech marked the beginning of an adjustment programme which involved four elements of trade liberalization. First, external finance was sought and obtained for balance of payments support to prevent an even larger drop in the volume of imports. Second, there was a substantial devaluation of 23 per cent in 1981. Third, producer prices for export crops were raised substantially. Finally and most importantly, a start was made on replacing all quantitative restrictions by tariffs.

This change in policy was not unproblematic. Theory and practice quickly began to diverge — for example, import bans which were supposedly abolished by the 1980 Finance Act continued to be used. The principle that quotas could be used to import any good within certain schedules was fought by the Ministry of Commerce (the target of lobbying activities), which wanted to retain item-specific quotas. To the extent that the first phase of the programme converted quantitative restrictions to 'equivalent' tariffs, protection was not reduced but simply took a different form. The more important second phase of the programme, which would lead to lower and uniform tariffs, had not been implemented by 1984.

The effect of the trade shocks on Tanzania was quite different. Given the system of import controls, declining foreign exchange availability reduced the supply of consumer goods both directly (as imports of these goods were virtually eliminated) and indirectly (as the production of consumer goods by foreign-exchange-starved domestic firms fell even further). The first liberalization of imports was a delayed response to the coffee boom of 1976 and 1977. Initially, import controls were not relaxed, in a deliberate attempt to build up reserves. This policy succeeded spectacularly. The foreign exchange revenues of the Bank of Tanzania increased by TSh

1 billion in 1977-78. Import controls were relaxed in 1978 (when the boom was in fact already over) and imports of consumer goods rose in that year to TSh 1,700 million (compared to TSh 1,152 million in the previous year).

In 1979 controls were tightened again and there was no change in the traditional priority ranking of imports of capital, then intermediate and — at the bottom — consumer goods. Imports of capital goods still increased in 1981 when all other categories of imports were falling. Subsequently, however, the government paid lip service at least to the idea of cutting the imports of capital goods in favour of those of intermediate inputs (including spare parts), not just for manufacturing but also for transport and agriculture. There were also indications that the government was willing to allocate imports, within a given priority category, to firms which were efficient users of foreign exchange. Yet to the extent that the import control policy was seen as an instrument for increasing agricultural exports the emphasis was on imports of intermediate inputs used in agriculture and in agro-processing industries, not on importing consumer goods to improve availability of such goods in rural areas. While the government was aware that cash crop production was constrained by shortages of consumer goods it believed that additional supply should come from domestic firms.

The National Economic Survival Programme (NESP), announced in 1981, acknowledged the need to reduce investment. The NESP policies for export rehabilitation included the use of export quotas (15 to 20 per cent of production) for industries producing exportables (a policy which made domestic shortages worse). Parastatal organizations, responsible for crop marketing, were allowed to keep 15 per cent of their export earnings to finance their own imports. In the meantime, Tanzania sought balance of payments support. An IMF agreement was concluded in September 1980 but was quickly suspended when ceilings on government expenditure were exceeded. When negotiations with the IMF were re-opened in 1982, the Fund demanded *inter alia*, increases in producer prices for export crops of 45 per cent in real terms, a devaluation from \$1 = TSh 10 to \$1 = TSh 25 or 35 and a doubling of interest rates. Agreement with the IMF on these three points was difficult and led to a suspension of lending by the World Bank and a cut back in aid programmes by bilateral donors. In June 1984, however, the government partially fulfilled certain of these requirements when the shilling was devalued to \$1 = TSh 17, producer prices were raised and food subsidies reduced.

During the 1970s domestic producer prices for export crops had been reduced by over one third in real terms. In 1981 the Government started to raise prices, a policy which continued during 1984. These increases came at the worst possible time — when farmers were already severely rationed. The government considered increasing the availability of consumer goods to peasants on several occasions. In 1976, however, it had been decided that the extra income peasants were earning as a result of the coffee boom would best be channelled into house improvements and the Board of Internal Trade (BIT) was instructed to increase the share of the coffee growing regions in the deliveries of building materials. One consequence was that dispatches by the BIT of corrugated iron sheets to the Kilimanjaro Region more than doubled in 1977. When the coffee boom was over, the importance of maintaining the increase in supplies to rural areas was stressed not just by outside observers but also in government circles. In fact, the Bank of Tanzania was instructed to allocate foreign exchange for this purpose for the first half of 1981. By then, however, the balance of payments position had become very much worse and the policy change was never implemented.

In summary, the Tanzanian government introduced some significant policy changes after 1978, but by 1984 it had not succeeded in restoring export growth through improved supplies of consumer goods to rural areas. The government's commitment to increasing the supply of consumer goods by raising domestic production of final goods rather than by importing them was likely to be slow and inefficient, while it was politically difficult to achieve the same result by reducing urban incomes. While these obstacles could have been overcome by providing external funds for additional imports of goods to be channelled directly to farmers, the willingness of both multilateral and bilateral donors to support such a programme was minimal.

External trade shocks, though damaging, were not the sole cause of the switch into a regime of pervasive rationing in Tanzania. The domestic policy stance — crop pricing, government expenditure and consumer price regulations — was itself sufficient to generate such a switch. The government chose to finance its ambitious expenditure programme through high implicit taxation of export crops, which curtailed export revenue. Meanwhile, price controls on maize reduced marketed output making it necessary to import maize to feed the urban population. The effect of these pricing policies, combined with the absolute priority given to public expenditure, was to produce severe scarcity of foreign exchange and, because of price controls, scarcity of consumer goods. Scarcity of foreign exchange induced a large premium between the black market and official exchange rates while scarcity of consumer goods induced a black market in consumer goods which generated large rents. The large rents created a portfolio problem for their owners which the wide exchange rate differential induced them to solve by holding foreign currency acquired through over-invoicing. The over-invoicing amounted to an avoidable worsening of the terms-of-trade which combined with the unavoidable deterioration to tighten the constraints upon the economy.

The problems were compounded by the fiscal implications of the coffee boom and its aftermath. Government revenue had been substantially increased by the boom and this was followed by a rise in public expenditure. The downturn in the coffee price and resulting squeeze on revenue were, however, not met by significant reductions in public expenditure. What had been windfall government expenditure was subsequently treated as a required claim on imports. This behaviour made it more likely that the economy would switch into a rationing regime.

In Chapter 3 it was argued that rural shortages would be implosive. It is difficult to document the intensification of shortages of consumer goods in rural Tanzania. To give one example, however, nationwide deliveries of Matsushita radios declined from 171,400 in 1977 to 59,000 in 1982, but for rural areas the decline was far steeper: from 134,100 to just 36,000. Accordingly, urban areas retained 60 per cent of former supplies, but rural areas retained only 27 per cent.

Long-run effects of intensified rural shortages on cash crop production were distinguished from short-run ones in Chapter 3. The long-run effect of rural shortages of consumer goods on cash crop production (and hence on the volume of exports) is strongly negative. As shortages become more severe farmers adjust by a combination of working less in total and (probably more importantly) by devoting relatively more of their working time to activities other than cash crop production. The short run effect, however, is muted. This is so because in the case of unpredictable rationing a decrease in availability of consumer goods may induce peasants to accumulate a larger money stock. The declining incentive to work on export crops will be partially offset by the need to work harder in order to accumulate the larger money stock.

Monetary data suggest that peasants did indeed increase their money holdings. Cash not held in banks increased from TSh 2.4 billion in 1977 to TSh 6.6 billion in 1981, a rise in the ratio to GDP from 11 to 24 per cent. Not all of this cash was held by individuals and, to the extent it was, some would have been held by urban households. For wage earners, however, there was less of an incentive to accumulate money because of the greater reliability of access to consumer goods in black markets. Black marketeers may well have accumulated large cash balances but these are unlikely to account for much of the increase if only because they had access to more attractive assets. Thus, peasants must account for the bulk of the change. Indeed, while only anecdotal evidence exists on the cash balances held by peasants in response to rationing, the government was so convinced of their magnitude that one of the reasons it objected to the decontrol of prices proposed by the IMF is that it would have generated massive inflation, because of these excess holdings. If velocity (defined as the ratio of money stock to GDP at current prices) had remained constant after 1977 then the money stock in 1981 would have been only 9.8 billion. In fact it was 8.9 billion higher than that, a difference which amounted to an astonishing 32 per cent of current-price GDP in 1981.

The build-up of money stocks contributed a 'honeymoon' phase to the adjustment process, which had probably come to an end by the early 1980s. While velocity fell from 3.2 in 1977 to 1.7 in 1980 it fell only slightly (to 1.6) in the next year. This suggests that between 1978 and the early 1980s the monetary adjustment muted the negative effect on export volumes of pervasive shortages of goods to purchase. The implications are first, that on unchanged policies even by 1984, the worst was yet to come, since Tanzania, unlike Kenya, had not then fully absorbed the external trade shocks because of its peculiar system of controls. Second, any analysis of trade liberalization in Tanzania must take into account the probable effects of the money stocks that had accumulated in response to rationing. Is there a sequence of liberalization which would have overcome these economic constraints without provoking intolerable political tensions? The next chapter considers possible adjustment programmes in the context of trade liberalization.

Chapter 6

Adjustment Programmes and Trade Liberalization

SHOCKS IN world trade may impair public sector decision-taking, inducing an irreversible ratchet-effect increase in public expenditure. This appears to have been an experience common to both Kenya and Tanzania. Since 'governments will be governments', temporary public windfalls become semi-permanent public commitments. This is, of course, economically avoidable: governments could stabilize the economy by adjusting foreign exchange reserves, or stabilize public revenue by adjusting tax rates. It may, however, be politically unavoidable.

At times of adverse external shocks the costs and benefits of liberalization become confused with the cyclical problems of retrenchment. Thus, 'structural adjustment' programmes typically attempt to combine the removal of distorting controls with the reduction in government expenditure. Since the prime motive for both government expenditure and controls in developing countries is often distributional — to confer benefits on favoured (generally urban) groups — the implementation of such programmes involves losses in real income for favoured groups and gains for disfavoured groups. This suggests that even in moderately distorted economies such as the Kenyan economy, the politically appropriate time to remove distorting controls is during a favourable external shock when rising public expenditure can be used to compensate politically powerful groups.

The other difficulty with the removal of distorting controls arises precisely because they are distorting and because they destroy information. In the process of moving the economy away from an efficient configuration they also leave doubt as to where — or what — that configuration is. The corollary is that it is usually rather difficult to design a liberalization programme that will take the economy towards greater efficiency. This point is usually neglected in discussions of liberalization because of an implicit assumption that the government's sole activity is to create distortions. Removing the distortions then effectively dispenses with the government and leaves the field free for market forces to locate the efficient configuration.

In practice the government must usually play a more positive part than this, at least if the exchange rate is to be managed, and it requires information to do so. For example, the first phase of the Kenyan liberalization programme required some knowledge of the level of tariffs that would provide protection equivalent to the dismantled quantitative restrictions. It could be argued plausibly that the foreign exchange crisis that led to the suspension of the programme was partly a consequence of a failure to get this level right.

Strategy for Trade Liberalization

What should the strategy have been? Consider the preliminary step of substitution of tariffs for quotas. Removal of quotas coupled with raising tariffs is always likely to be a risky policy. If the tariffs are over-estimated, the new regime is sustainable but more protectionist than the old; it will move the economy in the wrong direction. If they are under-estimated, the new regime will not be sustainable, there will be a relapse into quotas and, from the viewpoint of government, liberalization is likely to be discredited.

Were the import-competing sector competitive, quotas could be auctioned and the resulting prices used as measures of the necessary tariff rates. The condition was not met in East Africa. A better policy would be one of raising tariffs while maintaining quantitative restrictions. Only when the latter became slack would the government know that it had achieved a set of equivalent tariffs. It could then abolish them without risking a crisis, and move on to subsequent steps in its programme of liberalization in possession of much better information.

In a heavily distorted economy such as the Tanzanian economy an attempt to liberalize trade during an adverse external shock is still more liable to be economically ineffective and politically divisive. By combining a decline in the terms of trade with a boom-inherited increase in government expenditure, a negative shock can create a switch of regime into rationing. In a rationed environment the first priority of a stabilization programme is to reverse the regime-switch. This priority reflects both the inherently implosive tendency of a rationed peasant economy and the perverse response to many liberalization measures under rationing.

To escape from a rationed environment requires an improvement in availability of goods to peasants. Either this is financed externally (through aid) or it requires a redistribution from government expenditure and urban workers. In Tanzania the former course would have required an addition to non-project aid on a scale which donors were unlikely to countenance. While the limited success of much past project aid might appear to reinforce the case for a switch of funds to a recovery programme, it has in fact probably increased the resistance of donors to any new funding initiatives. At the same time, redistribution from government expenditure and urban workers would have required a politically powerful group to suffer losses while a politically weak group experienced gains, an implausible scenario. Further, an improvement in availability to peasants, though a necessary condition for a switch from rationing, would by itself generally not have induced a corresponding increase in marketed output in the short run and may even have reduced output despite a massive increase in imports, as peasants ran down their money balances.

The excess money balances of the rural community in Tanzania could have been dealt with in a number of ways which, in turn, could be grouped into those offering something in exchange for the excess balances and those that default on them through inflation or loss of currency value. The difficulties associated with devices in the first category make them impractical. The problem would be to find a good or an asset with two attributes. Not only must peasants want the good or asset but the economy must be capable of supplying it without using foreign exchange or other scarce inputs. Accordingly, currently produced goods are ruled out, leaving only financial assets (government bonds) and pre-existing real assets. It is not clear, however, that peasants would have voluntarily exchanged cash for bonds and even if they had done so, it would merely have deferred the problem. The only real asset they might have chosen to acquire was land but sales of state land to peasants would probably have proved politically infeasible in Tanzania. There appears therefore to have been no politically practical alternative to some measure of default.

Consequences of Liberalization

The precondition both for a powerfully positive short-run supply response by peasants to improved availability of goods for them to purchase is that peasant households should wish to increase their cash balances at the same time as they encounter improved availability of goods. Only with this combination is the long-run effect of improved availability of consumer goods on supply reinforced by the short-run cash-balance effect. Two possible devices are inflation and currency reconstruction. What are the relative merits of these two mechanisms of default by which peasant households could have been induced to increase their cash balances?

A currency reconstruction might have involved the exchange of new currency for old with limits on encashment *per caput*. It has two political advantages over an increase in prices. First, it would have fallen disproportionately upon black marketeers with large cash balances, a group unpopular with the government, and second, it is perhaps less likely to have induced expectations of subsequent inflation. The major advantage of an increase in the price level is that it would have afforded an opportunity to reduce the relative price of those goods or factors whose nominal prices were inflexible downwards but whose real prices were potentially flexible.

An increase in goods prices would directly have lowered the real price of crops and the real wage. A reduction in the real price of crops appears undesirable, for two reasons. First, it would have increased the magnitude of the distortions to be removed. In the process, it would have conveyed the wrong signals to peasants and thereby induced them to make long-term decisions, such as uprooting the coffee crop, which were irreversible and damaging. Second, there is some (unknown) reduction in crop prices beyond which crop output would have fallen. The risk of inadvertently triggering this response is too great to warrant a significant reduction in crop prices. Hence, an increase in the price of consumer goods would have needed to be matched by a rise in the price of crops, leaving urban real wages to decline. This would be equivalent to a devaluation.

Whether such a conjunction of improved goods availability for peasants and a decline in urban real wages would have been politically feasible in Tanzania probably depends upon the orders of magnitude involved. As discussed in Chapter 4, urban living standards could have been preserved through a fall in black market prices despite a fall in real wages. Since the reduction required in real cash balances would, however, have involved a doubling of the price level in the absence of currency reconstruction, powerful redistributions among wage earners would have been generated.

Whether a decline in urban living standards was desirable is doubtful. Whereas urban living standards were probably still above those experienced by most peasants they were almost certainly not above those which peasants would have experienced if the economy could have been switched into an unrationed state. Again a distinction must be made between policies designed to switch regimes and those designed to remove long-run distortions. From the point of view of removing distortions there seems to have been no case for a reduction in urban living standards; whether a reduction was necessary to switch regimes away from rationing depends upon the level of aid which might have been provided to fund such a switch.

Redistribution of Gains

The conjunction of full availability of goods to peasants and rationed availability to urban workers seems politically and economically unsustainable. Urban workers would have been able to undermine such a distributional arrangement politically and, economically, the urban black market would have diverted rural supplies. Thus the problem may not have been how to reduce urban living standards but how to prevent them rising (at a considerable cost in foreign exchange) as availability of goods improved nationally. The change in nominal wages needed to hold constant the living standards of urban workers as goods ceased to be rationed is readily calculable. Prices of goods needed to be increased precisely to that level at which the existing volume of consumer goods bought by urban workers had a value equal to the existing urban wage bill. This was not feasible, however, as long as the black market existed, since the consumption of black marketeers would have kept the availability of goods to workers below the wage bill. This has two important implications. First, when official prices are raised and total urban availability of consumer goods is kept constant, the profits of black marketeers are reduced, but the black market itself is only gradually eliminated. Once the official and black market prices become equal the quantity of goods formerly consumed by black marketeers accrues as a windfall gain to the government. Second, until this point is reached, the government must make goods available to the urban sector in excess of the real value of the wage bill. This 'over-supply' is equal to the consumption of the black marketeers, which will, however, be reduced by the effect of any currency reconstruction on their liquidity. Thus, an increase in official prices with money wages held constant can maintain the living standards of the average urban worker, while generating a windfall gain to the government.

Possible political obstacles to such a strategy were that two groups of urban households were vulnerable. First, an increase in price would have redistributed goods away from those who were succeeding in making an atypically high proportion of their purchases at official prices, a group in which the low paid may have been disproportionately represented. To offset this redistribution would have required a reduction in wage differentials and, since money wages were rigid downwards, this would have involved some increase in the minimum wage (though less than proportional to the increase in goods prices). Second, once workers were able to spend their wages on goods bought at official prices, their demand for the services of the informal sector would probably have been reduced. Informal sector workers would thus have faced both lower nominal incomes and higher official prices.

In the long run, there seems to be no way of avoiding a decline in living standards in the informal sector, for informal sector incomes can only be sustained by the permanent rationing of urban workers. It may well have been desirable, however, to reduce living standards gradually rather than abruptly. Such a gradual reduction would have required a gradual lessening in the severity of urban shortages. At the same time, rural shortages would have needed to be eliminated as rapidly as possible because of their economically implosive effects. Thus, to be economically viable an increase in the supply of goods must quickly eliminate rationing in rural areas, while, to be politically viable, the elimination of rationing in urban areas must be delayed if the urban households dependent for a living upon the informal sector are to be protected. Yet the conjunction of full availability of goods in rural areas and rationing in urban areas would have been unsustainable because the black market would have diverted rural supplies to urban consumers.

The dilemma could have been overcome by the temporary abandonment of nationally uniform official prices. In this case there would have been a currency reconstruction but no change in urban wages or official urban prices. In rural areas, however, both producer prices and official consumer prices would have been raised substantially and in proportion since it would not have been advisable to change relative prices as long as rural shortages persisted. These price increases would, if large enough, not only have sterilized the excess money balances but would also have reinforced the positive effect on coffee output of an aid-financed increase in rural availability (by reducing the value of the money balances of peasants below the new equilibrium level). In order to achieve the objective of preserving informal sector incomes the urban black market price level would have had to remain constant. This would have required official rural consumer prices to be equal to urban black market prices (adjusting for transaction costs) in order to prevent the diversion of rural suppliers to the urban black market. Such a policy package has two disadvantages. First, peasants might have expected still further price increases. Second, the urban black market could not have been eliminated.

Thus there were two alternative policy programmes that would have enabled a switch out of rationing to have been made. The choice between the two depended on the political constraints facing the government. The first would have included a devaluation (an equal increase in goods and crop prices), an increase in the urban minimum wage of a smaller magnitude, a currency reconstruction and foreign aid designed to ensure initial full availability of goods. The second, necessary only if the incomes of workers in the informal sector were to be protected, included an increase in official prices in rural areas only, possibly a currency reconstruction and again foreign aid.

If there was insufficient foreign exchange available to fund the transition from rationing, four policies would remain open to the government: (i) a still more severe currency reconstruction, (ii) a temporary decrease in real crop prices, (iii) a temporary decrease in urban living standards and (iv) a temporary decrease in government expenditure. The rationale for foreign aid was therefore not to bribe a recalcitrant government into making needed reforms but to avoid the need for policy changes which would need to be reversed once the economy was in unrationed equilibrium. Crop prices, urban living standards and government expenditure may well be unsustainably high in a rationed environment and yet be potentially sustainable in, or even too low for, an unrationed equilibrium.

Clearly, if the terms of trade were unchanged from the level at which the economy was driven into rationing then the initial configuration was unsustainable and public expenditure, for example, would need some permanent reduction. This was probably the case in Tanzania. The permanent reduction required, however, cannot be inferred from that level which would have been viable in an environment with rationing. Much government expenditure might have been productive (for example, road maintenance and health services) and the advantages of reducing it in order to provide consumer goods are ambiguous.

Maintaining an Unrationed Economy

Once the economy has been switched from a rationed to an unrationed regime a second stage of policy changes becomes appropriate, namely the revision of relative prices to those now optimal for public revenue or other objectives, given the switch in private incentives. With peasant supply no longer determined by expectations of rationing an increase in the price of export crops can be expected to induce an increase in output. In Tanzania the price to peasants was so far below the world price that it was probably even below that price at which government tax revenue would have been maximized.

The final stage of reform is concerned with reducing the vulnerability of the economy to a reversion into rationing. The starting point for such a reform is the recognition that in the future, as in the past, there will be periods of sharp and substantial reduction in export revenue resulting from shocks either to domestic supply or international demand.

Suppose now that the government has escaped from a rationed regime. There are three options open to it to ensure that such a reduction in export revenue does not induce a return to consumer rationing. First, price controls on consumer goods could be dismantled ensuring that prices of goods would rise to clear the market at times of scarcity. If price controls are to be retained, an alternative would be for government expenditure to be adjusted to accommodate consumer demand. In other words, instead of public expenditure pre-empting a fixed amount of foreign currency, thereby imposing sharp reductions in availability of goods to consumers when export revenue declines, private consumer claims should pre-empt the claims of government expenditure. Considerable downward flexibility in government expenditure would be required, since large and swift reductions would be necessary at times. Such flexibility would be politically difficult to achieve because much government expenditure is in the form of wages and salaries, but variations in public investment might make it feasible. If neither the abandonment of price controls nor the reversal of past priorities between public and private claims is regarded as acceptable, the only alternative is to accumulate large foreign exchange reserves. Both public and private claims could then be met during periods of reduced export revenue by running reserves down.

A policy of holding large foreign exchange reserves would impose long term costs since the holding of large reserves has an opportunity cost in the form of the higher returns which might have been earned had real assets instead of financial assets been accumulated. A more daunting drawback to the policy of holding large reserves is that such reserves would first have to be accumulated. A prolonged period of austerity, itself akin to a phase of abnormally low export revenue, would be required as a portion of foreign exchange earnings was withheld from both public and private claims. Not only does this require principled abstinence on the part of politicians, it is doubtful whether the economy could generate a significant balance of payments surplus even after an escape from rationing at 1984 levels of controlled consumer prices and public expenditure.

In short, while the avoidance of implosive rationing is analytically less complex than the escape from such a regime, none of the options open to economies currently vulnerable to the rationing 'trap' appear to be without political difficulty. All economies with an apparatus of extensive price controls and subject to large economic shocks are potentially vulnerable to consumer shortages even if the controlled prices are currently cosmetic. Hence this third stage of policy reforms is of relevance to a constituency far wider than those few countries to which the model of implosive rationing may currently be applicable.

Lessons from East Africa

While piecemeal policy changes can succeed in liberalizing trade in the control regime found in Kenya, they were liable to fail in the circumstances of the Tanzanian economy during the period 1978-84. Failure of such piecemeal policies is by no means confined to Tanzania which is typical of a group of African economies (for example, Ghana, Madagascar, and Mozambique). These heavily distorted economies have potentially most to gain from trade liberalization and are among the poorest nations in the world. Thus, in terms of human welfare they constitute a very significant problem for those wanting to secure liberalization.

That responses to liberalization may differ radically in such economies from the predictions of conventional analysis should not be surprising. Theories of rent-seeking behaviour in the presence of controls, developed since the mid-1970s, have uncovered a whole set of previously neglected costs of control regimes. The innovation of the present analysis has been to explore behaviour in response to shortages that are themselves a by-product of price controls. In the presence of such shortages some of the most frequently-recommended pricing reforms — for example, raising the price of cash crops, — can have perverse results. Furthermore, once a peasant economy enters an environment of shortages the economy has implosive tendencies because peasants are free to vary the labour expended on cash crops. This is why agriculture is usually the Achilles heel of command economies. In industrialized economies, in which shortages are also endemic, the same 'implosion' is less likely since industrial workers do not have the choice of reducing their incomes by working shorter hours. Finally, because of the monetary accumulation induced by the onset of shortages, the initial years of a control regime are a 'honeymoon' period as peasants work in exchange for paper. This very period does, however, subsequently lock the economy into shortages since an improvement in the supply of goods to peasants yields paper instead of extra crops.

A control regime may initially be cosmetic. Such, for example, was the present case with respect to price controls on consumer goods in Kenya. Either policy mistakes or trade shocks, however, can convert cosmetic price controls to effective price controls and generate shortages thereby. Once shortages emerge, the honeymoon phase of monetary accumulation disguises the catastrophic implosion to which the economy is headed. Yet, by the time the crisis becomes evident, the country is locked into a politically and economically intractable situation, the solution to which appears to require both considerable external funding and a careful sequencing of policy changes.

Appendix I

Optimizing Monetary Behaviour by Peasants

THE proposition argued in the text is complicated. This annex presents the simplest model in which the case can be formally articulated. A fuller model is also available from the authors.

1 Basics

To keep the model as simple as possible, the peasant household is assumed to produce the cash crop 'coffee' as a function of labour input subject to constant returns. One unit of coffee is produced by one unit of labour and is paid for one period in arrears. The price of a unit of coffee is the same as the price of a unit of the purchased commodity, 'soap'. We suppose that utility is intertemporally additive, with instantaneous utility at time t given by:

$$U = U(\underset{-}{L_t}, \underset{+}{G_t}) \qquad (1)$$

where G_t = the purchased commodity
L_t = labour on the cash crop.

The allocation of remaining labour between subsistence crop production and leisure is not studied in the model since it has no monetary implications.

2 Unrationed Equilibrium

If the commodity market is unrationed then, in equilibrium,

the household optimizes by choosing G* such that

$$\frac{\partial U}{\partial G^*_t} = -\frac{\partial U}{L_{t-1}} = -(1+r)\frac{\partial U}{\partial L_t} \qquad (2)$$

where r is the rate of interest, and enters (2) because of the delay in payment. The demand for money in the unrationed equilibrium will be set equal to expenditure, the simplest possible form:

$$M^* = G^* \qquad (3)$$

In (3) and subsequently, time subscripts are omitted since we restrict attention to stationary values. The budget constraint requires that income should equal expenditure, so

$$G^* = L = L^* \qquad (4)$$

(where * denotes unrationed equilibrium values).

3 Rationed Equilibrium in the Long Run

With prices unchanged, the quantity of 'soap' is now reduced and informally rationed so that the expected level of purchases of soap is less than the desired level:

$$E(G^R) < G^* \qquad (5)$$

where G^R = soap purchased under the rationing regime.

$E(\ )$ = the conditional mathematical expectation of the term in brackets.

In any particular period the actual purchases of soap may differ from the long run average, $E(G^R)$. However, it is assumed that soap is storable and that should the household have a run of bad luck such that its soap stocks fall to zero, it is able to borrow soap from other households (as long as its soap consumption does not exceed the sustainable level $E(G^R)$), which it returns once its stocks are positive. With this assumption, soap consumption in each period equals $E(G^R)$. This has implications for labour input and the marginal utilities of soap and leisure as depicted in figure 1.

Since the budget constraint will still bind, income will equal expected expenditure, so that:

$$E(G^R) = L = L^R \tag{6}$$

FIGURE A 1.1

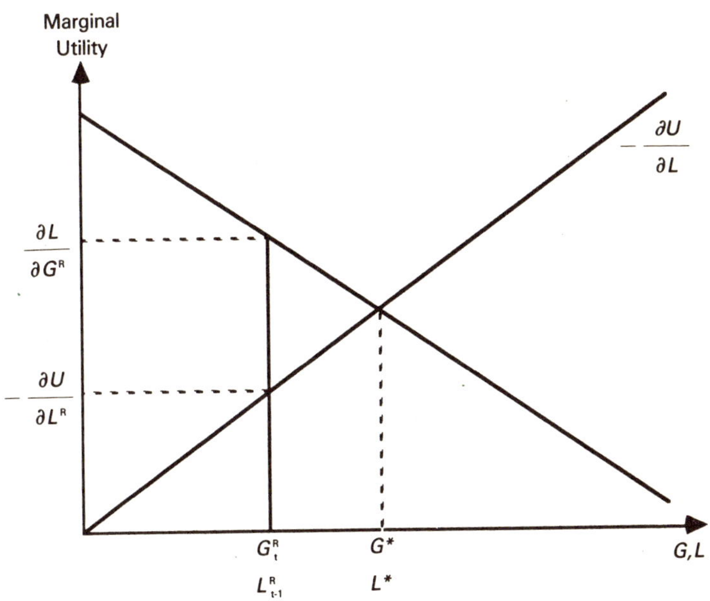

where L^R = optimal labour input under the rationing regime. Hence, the marginal utility of soap is higher and the marginal disutility of labour is smaller, than in the unrationed equilibrium. That is:

$$\frac{\partial U}{\partial G^R} \quad \frac{\partial U}{\partial G^*} \text{ and } -\frac{\partial U}{\partial L^R} < -\frac{\partial U}{\partial L^*} \tag{7}$$

The net benefit of a permanent one unit increase in the ration, $E(G^R)$, is therefore the discounted net present value of the extra utility from one more unit of soap per period minus the extra labour needed to pay for it:

$$\int_{t-0}^{\infty} \left(\frac{\partial U}{\partial E(G)^R} + \frac{\partial U}{\partial L^R}\right)/(1+r)^t\,dt = \frac{1}{r}\left(\frac{\partial U}{\partial E(G)^R} + \frac{\partial U}{\partial L^R}\right) \quad (8)$$

The utility of money in such a regime derives from the unpredictable access to goods. The access to goods depends upon the type of rationing regime encountered. In Tanzania there is no formal rationing system at the household level and availability is likely to be uncertain.

The household cannot purchase more than is available and cannot purchase more than it can pay for. Purchases are therefore subject to the double constraint:

$$G \leq M \text{ (the money stock constraint)} \quad (9)$$

and

$$G \leq G^A \text{ (the availability constraint)} \quad (10)$$

Which constraint is encountered depends on the level of the money stock and the probability distribution of the amount that is for sale $F(G^A)$. Since soap consumption is below its desired level it is never rational to choose not to make a purchase of available soap if money is available. Thus, one of the constraints (9) and (10) must always bind, so that either

$$G = G^A, \quad (11)$$

or

$$G = M \quad (12)$$

This creates a critical connection between the money stock held and the average value of goods consumption.

$$E(G^R) = \int_0^M G^A.F(G^A)dG^A + M.\int_M^{\infty} F(G^A)dG^A \quad (13)$$

Equation (13) states that expected purchases are the sum of two terms. The second term is the probability that the individual will be subject to the money stock constraint multiplied by the average purchase when this constraint binds, which is of course the money stock itself. The first term is most easily thought of, analogously, as the probability that the individual will be subject to the availability constraint multiplied by the average purchase when this constraint binds. Since the availability constraint can only bind when purchases are less than the money stock, average purchases must be less in this case. Hence, goods consumption is either equal to the money stock (if the money stock is the constraint) or less than the money stock (if goods availability is the constraint) so that expected goods consumption $E(G^R)$, is less than M. For all types of distribution, $F(G^A)$, the first order derivative of $E(G^R)$ with respect to the money stock is positive and the second order derivative is negative. Unfortunately, the RHS of (13) includes a censored distribution (that is, the part of the distribution below M) which is likely to lack analytically tractable properties.

Recall that since all prices are normalized, $\partial M/\partial L$ = unity and from (6) $\partial L^R/\ \partial E(G^R)$ = unity. The cost of an increment in the money stock is therefore the marginal disutility of labour, and for the money stock to be in a long run equilibrium, this marginal cost must equal the marginal benefit. The latter is equal to the change in goods purchases times the benefit from an increment in goods purchases, previously derived in (8). Hence, the equilibrium money stock, M^R, will satisfy:

$$-\frac{\partial U}{\partial L^R} = \frac{1}{r}\left[\frac{\partial E(G^R)}{\partial M}\left(\frac{\partial u}{\partial E(G^R)} + \frac{\partial u}{\partial L^R}\right)\right] \qquad (14)$$

4 Rationed versus Unrationed Equilibrium

Now consider how the optimal money stock changes in the long run if there is a change from a permanently unrationed to a permanently rationed commodity market. From (3), (5) and (13):

$$M^* = G^* > E(G^R) < M^R \tag{15}$$

This indicates that *a priori* $M^R \lesseqgtr M^*$ depending upon the utility function and $F(G^A)$. We will specify a simple instantaneous utility function, additively separable in L and G, in which both third order derivatives are set to zero. Thus:

$$\frac{\delta U}{\delta L} = -\alpha L \tag{16}$$

and

$$\frac{\delta U}{\delta G} = \beta - \gamma G \tag{17}$$

From (2), in unrationed equilibrium,

$$M^* = G^* = \frac{\beta}{\alpha + \gamma + \alpha r} \tag{18}$$

From (14) $$\frac{\delta E(G^R)}{\partial M} = \frac{\alpha r}{\frac{\beta}{E(G^R)} - \gamma - \alpha} \tag{19}$$

and from (13)

$$\frac{\delta E(G^R)}{\delta M} = \int_m^\infty F(G^A) dG^A \tag{20}$$

so in rationed equilibrium

$$\frac{\alpha r}{\frac{\beta}{E(G^R)} - \gamma - \alpha} = \int_m^\infty F(G^A) dG^A \tag{21}$$

Finally,

$$\frac{\delta\left(\frac{\delta E(G^R)}{\delta M}\right)}{\delta M} = -F(M) \qquad (22)$$

The geometric representation of the solution of (19), (20), (21) and (22) is shown in figure 2.

When $E(G^R) = G^* = M^*$, $\frac{\delta E(G^R)}{\delta M} = 1$, and the solution is traced out by the broken line. By contrast, a rationed equilibrium is traced out by the dotted line. Equation (19) defines the curve in the north-east quadrant; inspection of the equation shows that the curve is convex. The south east quadrant simply contains a 45° line, rotating the $E(G^R)$ axis. The curve in the south west quadrant is defined by equation (13) relating expected purchases to the money holding; evidently expected purchases in the rationed regime always fall short of G^*. Finally, the curve in the north west quadrant is defined by equation (20), that is, by the cumulative distribution of purchasing possibilities.

As drawn in Figure A1.2, the rationed money stock is greater than the unrationed money stock, but clearly a different distribution of purchasing possibilities could yield the converse case. Indeed, for a sufficiently severe ration (when schedule (20) is twisted far enough anti-clockwise around the vertical intercept) the money stock will be lower than when the goods are unrationed. However, computations using credible values and distributions suggest that the onset of rationing could well be characterized by an increase in the desired money stock.

FIGURE A1.2

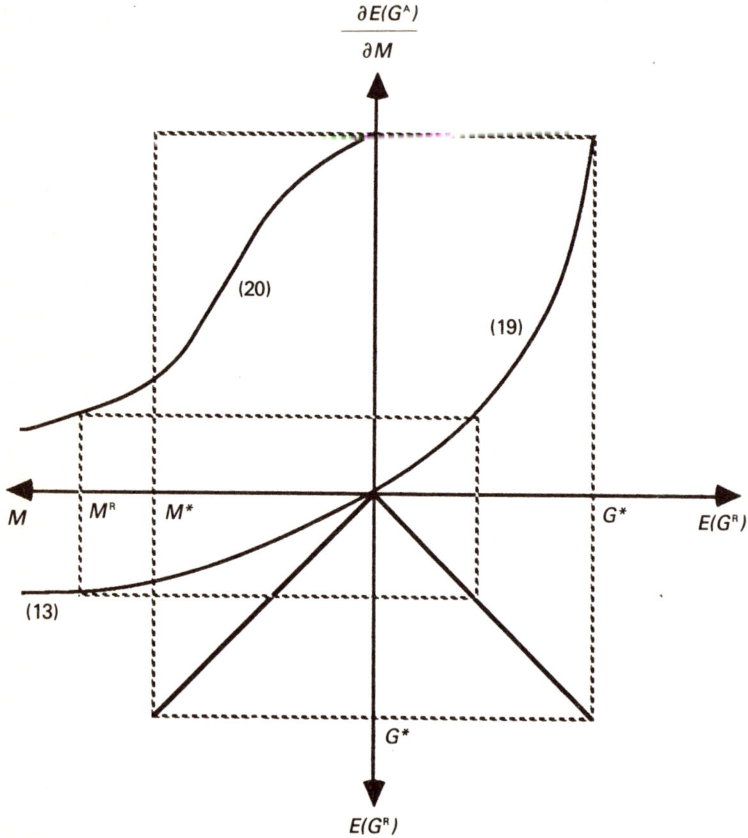

Appendix II

Macroeconomic Effects of Rural Rationing

IN FIGURE A2.1 the quantity of imported goods (or domestically produced consumer goods with a high import content) is measured along the horizontal axis and coffee production (that is, the volume of exports) along the vertical axis. The peasants' offer curve is the relation between their planned production of coffee and their planned consumption of imports in the absence of rationing. If, for example, the producer price were equal to AB/OA then peasants would choose point B. They would then plan to produce a quantity of OA of coffee which, if actually produced, would yield a volume AD of imports (the slope AD/OA of the foreign offer curve measuring the world price of coffee). Peasants would then consume AB and a quantity BD would be available for the urban sector. As drawn, the peasants' offer curve is parallel to the foreign offer curve at point B, hence that point represents the 'optimum', urban supplies (BD) being maximized. In this case the domestic price is lower than the world price: the 'optimal' coffee tax (BD/OA) is positive.

The exogenous urban claim on imported goods was now introduced.

In the diagram this is represented by a shift OE to the left of the foreign offer curve. Note that now only points in the shaded area (enclosed by the peasants' offer curve and the displaced foreign offer curve) are feasible in the sense that enough can be imported to satisfy the urban claim.

This is no longer possible if actual coffee output were to fall below the planned output OF. Suppose that, while the economy is initially at B, a bad harvest reduces exports to OG. Since the producer price remains the same as at B, the peasants revise downwards their intended consumption to GI. However, only GJ can now be imported, which after deducting the urban claim HJ, leaves only GH available for peasant

FIGURE A2.1

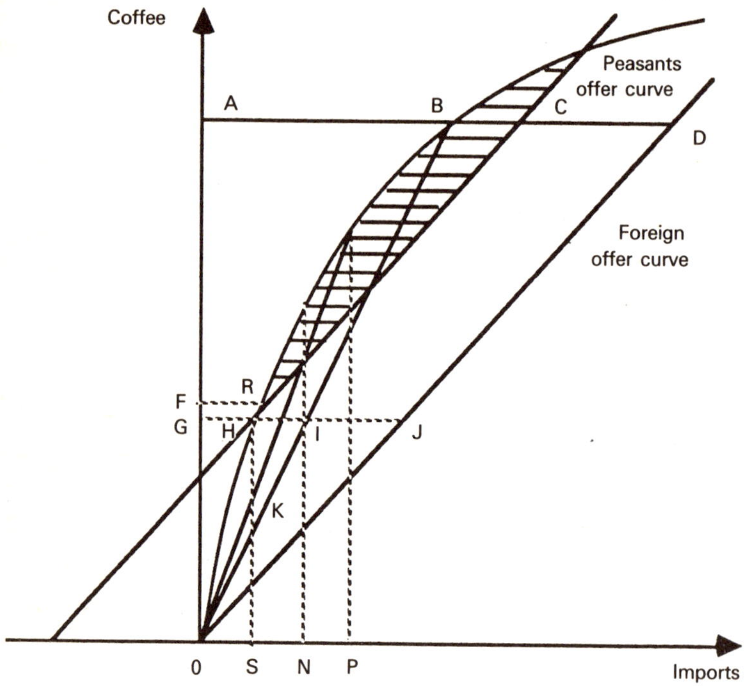

consumption. Hence peasants are rationed: they cannot realize their consumption. If peasants expect this availability to persist then they will in the long run reduce their income by producing less coffee such that their income is only sufficient to sustain available purchases. Hence they will gradually adjust their production so as to arrive at point K. However, as exports fall, rural availability is reduced even further: coffee output will continue to decline as long as the producer price is maintained and the urban claim on imports is honoured. The ambiguity of statements on the appropriateness of the level of the producer price in the case of rationing is illustrated by point L. Here rural availability equals ON. As long as this ration does not change, the producer price at L is too high: if the price were lower coffee production would increase until the farmers' original offer curve would be reached at the unrationed equilibrium point Q. On the other hand, reaching the 'optimum' B requires a producer price which is higher than at Q and, indeed, higher than at L. Therefore, whether the producer price at L can be called too high or too low depends on the extent, if any, to which price changes are accompanied by changes in availability.

Various departures from this optimum are now considered. First, it is shown that a reduction in coffee output due to a bad harvest or some similar shock can lead to an implosive contraction in output. Second, that such a contraction may initially be slow but will accelerate is also illustrated. Thirdly, it is shown that having got into a contractionary phase, there is some reduction in the coffee price which will raise output and arrest the contraction. A strategy of price reduction is dangerous, however, because if it is excessive the problem of implosive contraction can be compounded. Fourthly, a temporary windfall gain from higher world coffee prices which accrues entirely as government revenue and induces a permanent increase in government expenditure is considered.

So far, the possibility of a cumulative contraction in coffee output has been discussed implicitly in terms of certainty. When rationing is a matter of chance, the earlier discussion on optimum money holdings suggests that this process of implosion can be divided into two phases. In the first phase, as availability deteriorates desired money holdings rise so peasants temporarily produce more coffee than when their money stocks are at their chosen levels. Thus, starting at I, output may initially respond by falling from SH to a level considerably greater than SK. Hence, although the rationing point represents an unstable equilibrium the decline in output will initially be dampened. However, once availability deteriorates to the point at which peasants choose to reduce their money stocks the long-run tendency to implosive output reductions is accelerated by short run monetary dishoarding. Hence, once a price controlled economy stumbles into a regime of shortages which peasants expect to be sustained, output is subject to initially creeping but eventually rapid cumulative decline.

Starting at point L suppose the producer price is lowered; then, as we noted before, coffee production increases. This remains true until point Q is reached. The unrationed equilibrium point moves down along the peasants' offer curve from Q to R if the coffee price is lowered further. Beyond point R a price decrease is catastrophic since at prices below FR/OF no unrationed equilibrium exists at which sufficient coffee is produced to satisfy the urban claim. Hence the economy would collapse back into an implosively rationed regime.

Now consider the effect of a temporary windfall accruing entirely as government revenue which induces a permanent expenditure commitment. Suppose that in the initial situation both the domestic and the world price of coffee are equal to AB/OA. Hence coffee is not taxed, peasants choose point B, there is no urban claim and imports are entirely used for satisfying peasants' demand for consumer goods. Now the world coffee price temporarily improves from the slope of the ray OB to that of OD. At this new world price of coffee government revenue is BD, which initially finances EO of permanent commitments and BC of windfall expenditure. Given the permanent commitment EO, only if coffee ouput fell below OF would the economy switch into a rationing regime. However, if the BC windfall becomes a permanent commitment, the line EC shifts to the left through B, raising the minimum coffee output needed to avoid rationing.

List of References

THIS list contains only the more important references cited in the text. The reader should refer to the Notes and References at the end of each chapter for more complete bibliographical information.

DAVID BEVAN, PAUL COLLIER, JAN WILLEM GUNNING, ARNE BIGSTEN and P. HORSNELL, *Trade Shocks in Controlled Economies* (Washington: World Bank, 1986).

MARTIN E. BOND, 'Agricultural Responses to Prices in Sub-Saharan African Countries', *IMF Staff Papers*, Volume XXX, December 1983, pp. 703-26.

R.H. GREEN, 'Industrialization in Tanzania', in M. Fransmann (ed.), *Industry and Accumulation in Africa* (London: Heinemann, 1981), p. 90.

S. SHEPHERD, 'Marketing of Agricultural and Other Commodities in the Mbeya Region', a Report for the Food and Agricultural Organization, Dar es Salaam, 1982, p. 138.

Official Publications

KENYA ASSOCIATION OF MANUFACTURERS, East Africa Report on Finance and Industry, Nairobi, June 1977, p. 12.

List of Thames Essays

OCCASIONAL papers of the Trade Policy Research Centre are published under the omnibus heading of Thames Essays. Set out below are the particulars of those published to date.

1 GERARD and VICTORIA CURZON, *Hidden Barriers to International Trade* (1970), 75 pp.

2 T.E. JOSLING, *Agriculture and Britain's Trade Policy Dilemma* (1970), 52 pp.

3 GERARD and VICTORIA CURZON, *Global Assault on Non-tariff Trade Barriers* (1972), 44 pp.

4 BRIAN HINDLEY, *Britain's Position on Non-tariff Protection* (1972), 60 pp.

5 GEOFFREY DENTON and SEAMUS O'CLEIREACAIN, *Subsidy Issues in International Commerce* (1972), 75 pp.

6 GEORGE F. RAY, *Western Europe and the Energy Crisis* (1975), 68 pp.

7 THEODORE GEIGER, JOHN VOLPE and ERNEST H. PREEG, *North American Integration and Economic Blocs* (1975), 65 pp.

8 HUGH CORBET, W.M. CORDEN, BRIAN HINDLEY, ROY BATCHELOR and PATRICK MINFORD, *On How to Cope with Britain's Trade Position* (1977), 80 pp.

9 PETER LLOYD, *Anti-dumping Actions and the GATT System* (1977), 59 pp.

10 T.E. JOSLING, *Agriculture in the Tokyo Round Negotiations* (1977), 48 pp.

11 HARALD B. MALMGREN, *International Order for Public Subsidies* (1977), 80 pp.

12 DAVID ROBERTSON, *Fail Safe Systems for Trade Liberalisation* (1977), 80 pp.

13 SIDNEY GOLT, *Developing Countries in the GATT System* (1978), 42 pp.

14 THEODORE HEIDHUES, T.E. JOSLING, CHRISTOPHER RITSON and STEFAN TANGERMANN, *Common Prices and Europe's Farm Policy* (1978), 83 pp.

15 HANS BÖHME, *Restraints on Competition in World Shipping* (1978).

16 ROBERT E. HUDEC, *Adjudication of International Trade Disputes* (1978), 95 pp.

17 STUART HARRIS, MARK SALMON and BEN SMITH, *Analysis of Commodity Markets for Policy Purposes* (1978), 91 pp.

18 ROBERT Z. ALIBER, *Stabilising World Monetary Arrangements* (1979), 51 pp.

19 ROBERT L. CARTER and GERARD M. DICKINSON, *Barriers to Trade in Insurance* (1979), *Out of Print.*

20 GEOFFREY SMITH, *Westminster Reform: Learning from Congress* (1979), 59 pp.

21 W.M. CORDEN, *The NIEO Proposals: a Cool Look* (1979). *Out of Print.*

22 ROBERT E. BALDWIN, *Beyond the Tokyo Round Negotiations* (1979), 46 pp.

23 DONALD B. KEESING and MARTIN WOLF, *Textile Quotas against Developing Countries* (1980), 226 pp.

24 M.FG. SCOTT, W.M. CORDEN and I.M.D. LITTLE, *The Case against General Import Restrictions* (1980), 107 pp.

25 VICTORIA CURZON PRICE, *Unemployment and Other Non-work Issues* (1980), 63 pp.

26 V.N. BALASUBRAMANYAM, *Multinational Enterprises and the Third World* (1980), 89 pp.

27 T.E. JOSLING, MARK LANGWORTHY and SCOTT PEARSON, *Options for Farm Policy in the European Community* (1981), 96 pp.

28 DEEPAK LAL, *Resurrection of the Pauper-labour Argument* (1981), 82 pp.

29 ISAIAH FRANK, *Trade Policy Issues of Interest to the Third World* (1981), 76 pp.

30 GEOFFREY SHEPHERD, *Textile-industry Adjustment in Developed Countries* (1981), 68 pp.

31 CHARLES COLLYNS, *Can Protection Cure Unemployment?* (1982), 95 pp.

32 BRIAN HINDLEY, *Economic Analysis and Insurance Policy in the Third World* (1982), 68 pp.

33 HUGH CORBET, *Beyond the Rhetoric of Commodity Power*, second edition (forthcoming).

34 BRIAN HINDLEY and ERI NICOLAIDES, *Taking the New Protectionism Seriously* (1983), 98 pp. Second edition forthcoming.

35 KENT JONES, *Impasse and Crisis in Steel Trade Policy* (1983), 108 pp.

36 CHARLES PEARSON, *Emergency Protection in the Footwear Industry* (1983), 101 pp.

37 MARTIN WOLF, HANS HINRICH GLISMANN, JOSEPH PELZMAN and DEAN SPINANGER, *Costs of Protecting Jobs in Textiles and Clothing* (1984), 163 pp.

38 JOSÉ DE LA TORRE, *Clothing-industry Adjustment in Developed Countries*, (1984), 286 pp.

39 KENNETH W. CLEMENTS and LARRY A. SJAASTAD, *How Protection Taxes Exporters* (1984), 87 pp.

40 T.G. CONGDON, *Economic Liberalism in the Cone of Latin America* (1985), 130 pp.

41 INGO WALTER, *Barriers to Trade in Banking and Financial Services* (1985), 136 pp.

42 BASIL S. YAMEY, RICHARD L. SANDOR and BRIAN HINDLEY, *How Commodity Futures Markets Work* (1985), 80 pp.

43 DAVID GREENAWAY and BRIAN HINDLEY, *What Britain Pays for Voluntary Export Restraints* (1985), 178 pp.

44 ELLIOT SCHRIER, ERNEST NADEL and BERTRAM RIFAS, *Outlook for the Liberalisation of Maritime Transport* (1985), 94 pp.

45 GARY BANKS and JAN TUMLIR, *Economic Policy and the Adjustment Problem* (1986), 101 pp.

46 RICHARD PRYKE, *Competition among International Airlines* (1987), 113 pp.

47 JAMES RIEDEL, *Myths and Reality of External Constraints on Development* (1987), 111 pp.

48 DAVID BEVAN, ARNE BIGSTEN, PAUL COLLIER and JAN WILLEM GUNNING, *East African Lessons On Economic Liberalization* (1987), 72 pp.

49 ROLF J. LANGHAMMER AND ANDRÉ SAPIR, *Economic Impact of Generalized Tariff Preferences,* forthcoming (1987).

50 JIMMYE HILLMAN AND ROBERT ROTHENBERG, *Agricultural Trade and Protection in Japan,* forthcoming (1987).

51 DEEPAK LAL AND SARATH RAJAPATIRANA, *Impediments to Trade Liberalization in Sri Lanka,* forthcoming (1987).

52 ROMEO BAUTISTA, *Impediments to Trade Liberalization on the Philippines,* forthcoming (1987).

53 J.P. HAYES, *Economic Effects of Sanctions on Southern Africa* (1987), 100 pp.